IT'S A WONDERFUL LIFE

From the 1946 Liberty Film,
Distributed by Republic Pictures Corp.

IT'S A WONDERFUL LIFE

From the 1946 Liberty Film,
distributed by
Republic Pictures Corp.

Screenplay by Francis Goodrich, Albert Hackett
and Frank Capra
Additional scenes by Jo Swerling
Based on a story by Philip Van Doren Stern

IT'S A WONDERFUL LIFE. Published in 1986 by St. Martin's Press. Printed in the United States of America. For information, address St. Martin's Press, 175 Fifth Avenue, New York, N.Y. 10010.

Library of Congress Cataloging in Publication Data

Goodrich, Francis.
  It's a wonderful life.

  I. Hackett, Albert. II. Capra, Frank, 1897-
III. It's a wonderful life (Motion picture) IV. Title.
PN1997.I758 1986   791.43'72   86-6478
ISBN 0-312-43911-3 (pbk.)

First U.S. Edition

10 9 8 7 6 5 4 3 2 1

IT'S A WONDERFUL LIFE

From the 1946 Liberty Film,
Distributed by Republic Pictures Corp.

IT'S A WONDERFUL LIFE

CREDITS AND TITLES are SUPERIMPOSED OVER
beautiful moving clouds, CAMERA MOVEMENT
to give impression of RISING UP FROM the
earth. OVER THIS, full symphonic strength,
the MUSIC of Beethoven's Ninth, which,
since its theme is the Brotherhood of Man,
might very well form the motif of the over-
all score, winding up at the end with the
choral section of the final movement of the
symphony.

FADE IN

INT. BEN FRANKLIN'S OFFICE AND WORKSHOP - HEAVEN

CAMERA OPENS at entrance to this workshop. Joseph,
a sourpuss, flat-speaking, Ned Sparks type, enters.
He is dressed in smart business suit and carries a
rather large looseleaf folder. On his left breast is
a pair of shining, heavenly wings.

CAMERA TRUCKS AND PANS with Joseph as he goes by arbor
effect with openings in between through which can be
seen sunlit fields and heavenly vistas. The keynote
of these heavenly sets are no roofs, no walls, no
windows, no doors. It is externally day and
pleasant. The people, props, furniture, etc., are
all familiar to us. What little we see of Heaven must
want to make us go there.

Joseph comes into Ben Franklin's workshop and office.
Radio parts and various electronic devices are scattered
around. In the middle is a large, glass-topped table
at which Franklin (dressed and looking as before he
died) is examining some delicate electrical device.
The props and furniture are all familiar ones but the
office has no roof or walls. Arches or columns serve
for this purpose. Vines and flowers are in between
and distant vistas can be seen. Birds fly in and out.

Next to the table is a device with many dials and also
something that resembles a loud-speaker.

MED.SHOT. Joseph walks up to Franklin, who notices
him as he stops.

(CONTINUED)

                              FRANKLIN
                    Oh, hello, Joseph. New radar
                    equipment from down below --
                         (chuckling)
                    They're not far behind us down
                    there.

                              JOSEPH
                         (drily)
                    Yeah.

Joseph is deferential to Franklin, but his manner is
definitely tired, disillusioned and cycnical.

                              FRANKLIN
                    Trouble, Joseph?

                              JOSEPH
                    Looks like we'll have to send
                    someone down -- a lot of people
                    asking for help for a man named
                    George.

                              FRANKLIN
                    George who?

                              JOSEPH
                    Don't know, Mr. Franklin. The
                    prayers are coming from Bedford
                    Falls, New York.

                              FRANKLIN
                    Bedford Falls --

He switches on under-lighting on glass top table.
Another switch brings forth New York, lighted up.
Franklin looks for Bedford Falls.

                              FRANKLIN (cont'd)
                    Bedford Falls -- yes, here it is --
                    our territory all right. Are the
                    prayers sincere, or are they the
                    "gimme" type?

                              JOSEPH
                    I'm getting so I can' tell. Why
                    don't you listen in, sir?

Franklin turns to mechanism alongside, that looks like
loud-speaker, and revolves a dial until he comes to
Bedford Falls. An overlapping murmur of prayers are
heard.

                              (CONTINUED)

                              VOICES
                    Oh Lord, please help my son,
                    George -- he needs You...

                    George is a good guy. Please,
                    God, give him a break...

                    I love him, dear God. Watch over
                    him tonight.

                    Please, God -- something's the
                    matter with Daddy...

Franklin switches off prayers.

                              FRANKLIN
                    It's George Bailey. What day is
                    it down there?

                              JOSEPH
                    Christmas Eve.

                              FRANKLIN
                    Hmmm. Tonight's his crucial
                    night. Let's see what he's doing
                    now.
                         (turns some knob; then
                          they both peer into glass
                          top desk as if they see
                          something)
                    You're right. We must send
                    someone down quick. Whose turn is it?

                              JOSEPH
                    That's why I came in to see you, sir.
                    It's 1163-B's turn.

                              FRANKLIN
                    Oh -- Clarence. We've passed him
                    up right along, haven't we? Hasn't
                    got his wings yet, has he?

                              JOSEPH
                    Well, you know, sir, he's got the
                    I.Q. of a rabbit.

                              FRANKLIN
                    Yes, but he's got a good heart.
                    George needs somebody with a heart.

                              JOSEPH
                    You know what happened the only time
                    we did send him down -- he got lost.
                    We finally found him on a merry-go-
                    round in Coney Island.

                                        (CONTINUED)

                              FRANKLIN
                          (thinking)
                    But that was New York City. This
                    is a small town. He's got the
                    faith of a child -- simple. Yes,
                    that'll reach George quicker than
                    a high I.Q. Joseph, let's take a
                    chance. Send for Clarence.

                              JOSEPH
                    Poor George Bailey.
                          (toward door)
                    Johnny!

A young Page pops in at door.

                              JOSEPH (cont'd)
                    Ask 1163-B to come in.

                              PAGE
                    Right away, Mr. Kearns...
                    Call for 1163-B!...Call for 1163-B!

The page exits.

                              JOSEPH
                          (to Franklin)
                    Of all the billions of people up
                    here, George Bailey has to draw
                    Clarence.

CLOSEUP - parrot at entrance. A parrot is on a stand
at entrance. It starts laughing and making funny noises.

MED. SHOT - entrance. Johnny and Clarence. Page is
dressed like "Johnny" of Philip Morris fame, except
that he is a colored boy.

Clarence is a wide-eyed, childlike sort of man past
fifty. He evidently belongs to the Seventeenth Century
for he is dressed in the pre-Revolutionary American
clothes of a moderately well-to-do shopkeeper.

As he comes in, he is nervous, eager and out of
breath. He still has his thumb in a copy of "Tom
Sawyer" which he has been reading. CAMERA STAYS WITH
him as he goes up to Joseph and Franklin.

CLOSEUP - Joseph and Franklin. Franklin looks Clarence
over with thoughtful interest. Joseph makes a face
as if he smelled something.

CLOSEUP - Clarence.

                            (CONTINUED)

                         CLARENCE
                    (breathing hard and
                     tripping over something)
               You sent for me, sir?

                         JOSEPH
                    (to Franklin)
               See what I mean? He couldn't
               fight his way out of a paper bag.

                         FRANKLIN
               Yes, Clarence, we sent for you.
               There's a man in trouble.

                         CLARENCE
                    (beaming)
               Splendid! Why, that's fine!

                         FRANKLIN
                    (sternly)
               I said trouble.

Franklin turns on speaker again. This time we hear
George's voice, with a bar and juke-box background.

                         GEORGE'S VOICE
               But if You're up there, God --
               and You can hear me -- show me the
               way. I'm at the end of my rope,
               dear God. Show me the way.

Franklin shuts it off.

                         FRANKLIN
               At exactly 10:45 tonight, earth-time,
               that man will be thinking seriously
               of throwing away God's greatest
               gift --

                         CLARENCE
               Tch, tch, tch. His life.
                    (consults his
                     watch)
               Then I have only a half hour to dress.
               What are they wearing now?

                         FRANKLIN
               You will spend that time learning
               some of the details of George
               Bailey's life.

                         CLARENCE
               Of course. Of course. I'm sure I
               can help him, sir. My friends used
               to say I was so gay I made them forget
               their troubles.

                                        (CONTINUED)

                        FRANKLIN
          You're supposed to do more than
          entertain him. You're supposed
          to make him <u>understand</u> --

                        CLARENCE
                (humble and
                 moved)
          Thank you, sir. I'll do my best.
          I appreciate your trust in me.

                        FRANKLIN
          I'll leave you with Joseph. He'll
          give you the details.
                (turns to go)
          We mustn't fail George Bailey.

                        JOSEPH
                (going to desk and
                 beginning to
                 operate dials)
          Poor George. If this works, I'm
          going to believe in fairies from
          now on.

                        CLARENCE
                (to Franklin,
                 who is leaving)
          Sir.

Franklin turns.

                        CLARENCE (cont'd)
          If I should accomplish this mission
          -- do you think, sir -- I mean --
          might I perhaps win my wings?
          I've been waiting nearly two
          hundred years now, sir -- and
          people <u>are</u> beginning to talk.

Joseph grimaces. Franklin muses thoughtfully.

                        FRANKLIN
          Clarence, you do a good job of
          this, and I'll see that you get
          your wings.

                        CLARENCE
          Oh, thank you, sir -- thank you.

                        FRANKLIN
          What's that book you've got there?

                         CLARENCE
          "The Adventures of Tom Sawyer."

                         FRANKLIN
          Clarence, by golly, I think you're
          going to make it!

                         JOSEPH
               (to himself)
          Not for my dough.

Franklin leaves.

                         CLARENCE
               (to Joseph)
          It's been too humiliating, you
          know. I've sat there and watched
          young fellows who've been here
          only a hundred years being pushed
          up ahead of me. I've had some
          ugly thoughts on the subject.
          -- Like I came to the wrong place
          or something.

                         JOSEPH
          You've got to be smart to get in
          the other place.

Joseph turns some knobs and glass top elevates to
a vertical position.

                         CLARENCE
          Where does this George Bailey
          live?

                         JOSEPH
          Beford Falls, New York State.
               (picks up phone)

                         CLARENCE
          Oh, then maybe I can go to Coney
          Island again.

                         JOSEPH
          You do, and we leave you there this
          time.
               (into phone)
          Run JB X 23475, Series NN2.

                         CLARENCE
          What now?

                                        (CONTINUED)

                         JOSEPH
Sit down here. You're supposed
to go down and help Beorge Bailey,
aren't you?

                         CLARENCE
Why, yes -- I --

                         JOSEPH
Well, then you want to know what
makes George tick, don't you?

                         CLARENCE
Well, naturally. I --

                         JOSEPH
Well, relax and look at the screen.
It's coming on now. See the
town?

                         CLARENCE
          (squinting, but
           not seeing anything
           but glass table top)
Oh yes, yes --
          (honestly, turning
           to Joseph)
I don't see a thing -- where?

                         JOSEPH
Right there in front of you.

                         CLARENCE
          (seeing
           nothing)
Now, honestly -- you see anything?

                         JOSEPH
You mean to tell me you don't --
aw, I keep forgetting you haven't
got your wings yet. Poor George.
Now, look, take it easy, I'll help
you out. Concentrate. Put your
mind to it. Begin to see something?

                         CLARENCE
          (in wonderment)
Yes, yes! I do see something!
This is amazing.

                         JOSEPH
When you get your wings you'll
see it all by yourself.

                              (CONTINUED)

                          CLARENCE
          Oh really? Wonderful! That's
          what it means to earn your wings.

                          JOSEPH
          Look at the screen.

CLOSE SHOT - The screen. The thing on the screen,
fuzzy and obscure, comes into clear focus and is
revealed as a soot-stained, snow-covered sign which
reads:

                    NO TRESPASSING
              Violators will be prosecuted to
                the full extent of the law

                    HENRY F. POTTER

CAMERA, PULLING BACK, reveals the sign is on the edge
of an empty, junk-filled lot. It is snowing. CAMERA
STARTS MOVING, PASSING BY the most abject and squalid
sort of houses. In the bitter desolation of winter,
the hovels look more wretched than ever, and the
glimpse we get of the people of the section, shivering
in their shabby, inadequate garments, indicates we
are definitely on the wrong side of the tracks. The
scene is in striking contrast to the sunny vistas of
Heaven we have been witnessing.

The MOVING CAMERA PASSES several "TO RENT" signs on
the miserable dwellings, and each of the signs bears
the name HENRY F. POTTER. The PROGRESS of CAMERA is
leisurely, ruthless, in its exposition of this cold
and bitter hell-on-earth.

INT. PROJECTION ROOM - HEAVEN - MUSIC - DAY

TWO SHOT. Clarence and Joseph.

                          CLARENCE
          Where in the world is that?

                          JOSEPH
          Town called Bedford Falls.

                          CLARENCE
          What an awful place!

                          JOSEPH
          This is only the slum section.
          It's called Potter's Field.

                          CLARENCE
          Why?

                              JOSEPH
          It's owned by a man named Potter.

                              CLARENCE
          Must be an awfully poor man.

                              JOSEPH
          He's the richest man in town.

                              CLARENCE
          Then why is the place so ugly
          and cheerless?

                              JOSEPH
                    (a bit impatiently)
          If you'll only keep your eyes
          and ears open --

                              CLARENCE
          Excuse me.

He relaxes into the chair and glues his eyes on screen.

CLOSE SHOT - The screen. As CAMERA MOVES UP CLOSE to
it, FRAMING OUT the screen itself, we are on:

EXT. TOWN - ON RIGHT SIDE OF TRACKS - MUSIC - DAY

MOVING SHOT. The CAMERA NOW MOVES PAST grounds
enclosed within a tall, spiked, iron fence. As it
PROGRESSES TOWARD the entrance, we get a glimpse of
several signs:

               NO TRESPASSING

               BEWARE OF DOGS

               KEEP OUT

In the b.g., presently, we discern through the falling
snow a gaunt and forbidding house, bleak in the winter
landscape.

INT. PROJECTION ROOM

TWO SHOT - Clarence and Joseph.

                              CLARENCE
          Is that a prison?

                              JOSEPH
          It's the home of Henry F. Potter.

                                        (CONTINUED)

                              CLARENCE
               Why have they got an iron fence
               all around it? Is he violent?

                              JOSEPH
                    (exasperated)
               If you'll stop asking questions --

                              CLARENCE
                    (contritely)
               I'm sorry.

He settles back in his seat again, watching.

INT. PROJECTION ROOM

MED. SHOT - screen. As CAMERA MOVES UP CLOSE we
are on:

EXT. ROAD - OUTSIDE POTTER HOME - MUSIC - DAY

FULL SHOT. The MOVING CAMERA GOES UP TO the house,
looks in at a window, and STOPS. When CAMERA STOPS,
the MUSIC stops also, right in the middle of a passage.
The simultaneous stoppage of sound and motion is
dramtic. Gradually we hear the pleasant distant shrieks
of children at play.

CLOSE SHOT - Potter. Through the window we see a man
of about fifty, clad in a dressing gown. His face is
ravaged and bitter.

INT. PROJECTION ROOM - DAY

TWO SHOT -   Joseph and Clarence.

                              CLARENCE
               Who is that? George Bailey?

                              JOSEPH
               No. Henry F. Potter.

                              CLARENCE
               I don't like him.

                              JOSEPH
               You're not supopsed to.

CLOSE SHOT - Potter. His face reacts vengefully as
he watches kids playing.

MEDIUM SHOT - DAY - WINTER

About eight boys ranging from nine to twelve have a
skate run that attempts to imitate a ski run. Starting
from the top of a small knoll they slide down in large
shovels on the flat ice of a creek bed.

The idea is to see who can slide the farthest. The
boys all wear some same distinctive head-piece which
will give the idea of a tightly knit little boy's club.

George Bailey is the Master of Ceremonies at the bottom
of the slide. He has a small megaphone through which
he calls out the names of the contestants and the
length of their slide. He marks the spot where each
contestant finishes.

Sitting on a couple of Potter's "No Trespassing" signs
are two small five-year olds who constitute the audience
for this magnificent spectacle. George exhorts them
to cheer or boo as the occasion demands.

A small bridge spans a creek bed nearby. On this bridge
stands Mary, calling her brother.

At the end of the flat ice where the boys pull up is the
thin ice.

Alongside the whole run is a strong barbed wire fence
which resembles a prison fence. Sprinkled freely along
its length are signs reading "No Trespassing."
"Trespassers will be prosecuted to the full extent of
the law...Henry F. Potter," and "Beware of Dogs."

MED. SHOT - TOP OF KNOLL

The kids are at the start mark. George is ready to
start.
                         GEORGE
                    (through his
                     megaphone)
          For the Championship of Bedford Falls
          and all points West! The one and
          only George Bailey will make the
          first slide!

So saying, he starts down the knoll and slides onto
the ice, handling his shovel like a champion. The
rest of the scene he plays at foot of the knoll.

CLOSEUP - KNOLL

                    SAM WAINWRIGHT
          Hee, haw - Mary -- Hee Haw!
            (he waggles his hands
             at his ears)

CLOSEUP - MARY

                    MARY
          You're just a big jackass, Sam
          Wainwright. And you're a bigger
          jackass, George Bailey. Twice as
          big. Marty! Marty!

CLOSEUP - GEORGE

He picks up snowball and heaves at Mary. It hits
her in the face.

CLOSEUP - MARY

Mary gets hit with snowball. She crys but still stands
there yelling for Marty.

CLOSEUP - GEORGE

He laughs at Mary and calls for next contestant.

                    GEORGE
          Next comes the great Sam
          Wainwright, nearest thing to a
          human jackass - let's go!

CLOSEUP - KNOLL

Sam Wainwright "Hee haws" and takes off. He does a
comedy slide, spinning his shovel around on the ice.

CLOSEUP - GEORGE

                    GEORGE
          Next on the program, the great
          brain, Ernie Bishop!

CLOSEUP - KNOLL

Ernie Bishop takes off and beats George's mark.

CLOSEUP - GEORGE BAILEY

Marks his finish mark with a marker.

>   GEORGE
> The most terrific slide of all
> time! George Bailey - his mark...
>   (turns to the
>   two little kids)
> Applause, applause!
>   (through his
>   megaphone)
> Next, the great and handsome Marty
> Hatch.
> Applause, applause!

CLOSEUP - MARY ON BRIDGE

>   MARY
> Marty! Mom wants you, Marty!

CLOSEUP - TOP OF KNOLL - MARTY HATCH

>   MARTY
> Oh, that sister of mine! Go on
> home, will you, Mary!

Marty slides down. His mark is short of George's.
He, too, finishes gracefully.

CLOSEUP - MARY

>   MARY
> Marty! Moma wants you! Marty!

CLOSEUP - MARTY

>   MARTY
> I'll kill her if she don't stop.

CLOSEUP - GEORGE

>   GEORGE
> Go on home, will you, Mary. Wanna
> break up the Olympic games?

CLOSEUP - GEORGE

                    GEORGE
         And here comes the scare-baby, my
         kid brother, Harry Bailey. Applause!

CLOSEUP - KNOLL

Harry Bailey, a lad of nine, obviously frightened,
takes his place.

                    HARRY
         I'm not a scare-baby!

He takes off, does a terrific slide, but his shovel
seems to gain momentum on the slick ice, and he
slides on past the safe area and breaks through the ice.

CLOSEUP - GEORGE

                    GEORGE
         I'm coming, Harry. Hang on!

George flies to the break and dives in. He comes up
with Harry and holds him up while he trys to hang onto
the breaking edges.

                    GEORGE
              (to the others)
         Make a chain! Make a chain!

The other boys lie down and grab each other's ankles.

CLOSEUP - MARY

She is admiring her hero, George.

CLOSEUP - POTTER AT HIS WINDOW.

Potter has evidently seen the whole episode.

                    POTTER
              (to his goon)
         Serves them right, the noisey
         brats.

                    FADE OUT

FADE IN

EXT. MAIN STREET, BEDFORD FALLS - SPRING AFTERNOON

CLOSE (MOVING) SHOT. The same kids, arms interlocked
and still whistling "As I Was Walking Down The Street"
are monopolizing the sidewalk as they approach Gower's
Drugstore. As in the winter sequence they wore
identical hats, indicating a fraternal kinship, so
now they wear baseball caps. The whistling line of
kids comes to a stop in front of Gower's. The
drugstore is old-fashioned and dignified with jars
of colored water in the windows and little else. As
the kids stop:

                    KIDS
               (ad libbing at
                doorway)
          Tell you how it comes out! Hit
          a homer for you! Etc., etc.

                    GEORGE
          S'long.

                    SAM
          Go to work, you slave.
               (makes his
                familiar gesture)
          Hee-haw!

George crosses to cigar lighter, crosses fingers,
closes eyes, and with other hand snaps lighter.

                    GEORGE
          I wish I had a million dollars!
               (light flares)
          Hot dog!

INT. DRUGSTORE - DAY

As George comes in the door, he calls out pleasantly
toward the back prescription room.

                    GEORGE
          It's me, Mr. Gower, George Bailey.

                    GOWER'S VOICE
               (gruffly)
          You're late.

                    GEORGE
          Yes, sir.

                              (CONTINUED)

As he starts to take off his coat and go behind the soda fountain, he stops, looking off.

WIDER ANGLE - inlcuding Mary Hatch. She is standing near the candy counter, her schoolbooks in her hand, dumbly looking at him. George goes on to get a big apron from behind the counter. Violet Bick comes in by another door. She is the same height as Mary and the same age, but she is infinitely older in her approach to people.

                    VIOLET
              (with warm
               friendliness)
          Hello, George.
              (then, flatly,
               as she sees Mary)
          'Lo, Mary.

                    MARY
              (primly)
          Hello, Violet.

George regards the two of them with manly disgust. They are two kids to him, and a nuisance. He starts over for the candy counter.

                    GEORGE
              (to Violet)
          Two-cents' worth of shoelaces?

                    VIOLET
          She was here first.

                    MARY
          I'm still thinking.

She starts over toward the soda fountain.

                    GEORGE
              (to Violet)
          Shoelaces?

                    VIOLET
          Please, Georgie.

George goes over to the candy counter. Violet moves over to Mary.

                              (CONTINUED)

CLOSE SHOT - Mary and Violet. Mary is absorbed in
studying the names of the sodas listed on the wall.
Violet speaks to her softly.

                         VIOLET
               He's cute, isn't he?

                         MARY
               Who?

                         VIOLET
               Georgie.

                         MARY
               He's just a show-off.

                         VIOLET
                    (looking off at George)
               I like him.

                         MARY
               You like every boy.

                         VIOLET
                    (happily)
               What's wrong with that?

                         GEORGE'S VOICE
               Here you are.

                         VI
                    (on stool at counter)
               Help me down.

                         GEORGE
                    (disgusted)
               Help you down?

He goes to cash register. Vi jumps down and starts
out. She and Mary stick tongues out at each other.

WIDER ANGLE - including George. George gives Violet
a handful of licorice strips. Violet gives her money
to him, bites off a length of the "shoelaces" and
gives Mary a friendly slap on the back with them.
George watches her, disgusted.

                         VIOLET
                    (the vamp)
               Goodbye Georgie.

                         MARY
                    (mimicking)
               Goodbye, Georgie!

                              GEORGE
                         (to Mary
                          businesslike)
                    Made up your mind yet?

                              MARY
                    I'll take chocolate...

George starts for the chocolate.

                              MARY (cont'd)
                    No...strawberry...
                         (then, in an agony
                          of indecision)
                    No...chocolate.

                              GEORGE
                    With coconut?

                              MARY
                    I don't like coconuts.

                              GEORGE
                    You don't like coconuts? Say
                    brainless, don't you know where
                    coconuts come from?

He pulls out National Geographic Magazine.

                              GEORGE (cont'd)
                    Lookit here -- from Tahiti -- Fiji
                    Islands, the Coral Sea!

                              MARY
                    A new magazine -- I never saw
                    it before.

                              GEORGE
                         (archly)
                    Of course you never. Only us
                    explorers can get it. I've been
                    nominated for membership in the
                    National Geographic Society.

                              MARY
                    What's that?

                              GEORGE
                         (exasperated)
                    What's that? For the love of Pete,
                    don't you realize what that means?
                    Know where they send us? Out to the
                    ends of the earth -- up in the balloons,
                    down into the seas, exploring and
                    everything.

                                        (CONTINUED)

He leans down to scoop out the chocolate ice cream,
his deaf ear towards her. She leans over, speaking
softly.

                    MARY
          Marty says you can't hear on one
          ear -- is this the ear you can't
          hear on?

He doesn't hear her. Unconsciously he talks right on.

                    GEORGE
          I'm going out exploring some day,
          you watch. And I'm going to have
          a couple of harems, and maybe
          three or four wives. Hot dog!

He bends down again. Mary leans closer and speaks
softly into his deaf ear.

                    MARY
          George Baily, I'll love you till the
          day I die.

She draws back quickly and looks down, terrified at
what she has said.

                    GEORGE
               (straightening up)
          What?

                    MARY
          I said I'd -- I'd like coconut.

                    GEORGE
          Make up your mind, female.

He turns back to counter, whistling "As I Was Walking
Down The Street."

ANOTHER ANGLE - taking in entrance to prescription
room at end of fountain. Gower comes to the entrance.
He is bleary-eyed, unshaven, chewing an old unlit
cigar. His manner is gruff and mean. It is evident
he has been drinking.

                    GOWER
          George! George!

                    GEORGE
          Yes, sir.

                    GOWER
          You're not paid to be a canary.

                                        (CONTINUED)

                              GEORGE
          No, sir.

He turns back to counter to spoon out some coconut,
when he notices an open telegram on the coconut
container near the cash register. He is about to
toss it aside when he starts to read it.

INSERT THE TELEGRAM. It reads:

          "We regret to inform you that your
           son, Robert, died very suddenly
           this morning of influenza.
           Everything possible was done for
           his comfort. We await instructions
           from you.

                              EDWARD MELLINGTON
                              Pres.HAMILTON COLLEGE."

BACK TO SHOT. George puts telegram down. A goodness
of heart expresses itself in a desire to do something
for Gower. He gives the ice cream to Mary without
comment and sidles back toward Gower.

                              GEORGE
          Mr. Gower, do you want something --
          anything?

There is only a grunt from Gower in answer. George
wipes his hands and goes to the back, looking in at
the jammed prescription room.

INT. GOWER'S DRUGSTORE - BACK ROOM

Gower, drunk, is intent on his work.

                              GEORGE
                         (sympathetically)
          Anything I can do back here?

                              GOWER
          Nope.

                              GEORGE
          Want a fresh cigar?

                              GOWER
          Nope.

                              (CONTINUED)

George looks curiously at Gower, realizing that
he is quite drunk. He looks over at the bottle from
which Gower is taking powders for the capsules. He
moves in stealthily for a closer look. Gower fumbles
and drops some of the capsules to the floor.

                    GEORGE
          I'll get them, sir.

He picks up the capsules and gives them to Gower.
Then, behind Gower's back he turns the powder bottle
to have a better look. Its label has a skull and
bones on it. George stands still, horrified.

                    GOWER
               (growling)
          You're in the way, George.

He waves George aside, spills something else, takes
his wet cigar, shoves it in his mouth and sits in an
old Morris chair in the b.g.

                    GOWER (cont'd)
          Wrap the capsules...go to Mrs. Blaine's
          ....waiting for them.

                    GEORGE
          Yes, sir.

Gower sits, head down, chewing the dead cigar. George
picks up the capsule box, not knowing what to do or
say. His eyes go, harassed, to the bottle labeled
poison. George's fingers fumble.

                    GEORGE (cont'd)
          They have the diptheria there,
          haven't they?

                    GOWER
          Ummm.

Gower stares moodily ahead, sucking his cigar. George
turns to Gower, the box in his hand.

                    GEORGE
          Is it a charge, sir?

                    GOWER
          Um - charge. Get going!

                    GEORGE
          Yes, sir.

George comes out into the main room. He sees Mary
watching him. Instinctively he'd like to confide in
her.

                         GEORGE (cont'd)
              Mary, I --
                    (abruptly)
              Watcha looking at me for?
              Why don't you go home?

Mary stares in bewilderment. Behind her George sees
a Sweet Caporals ad which says:

INSERT: "ASK DAD HE KNOWS."

BACK TO SHOT: With an inspiration, George dashes out
of door and down the street. Mary follows him out
with her eyes.

EXT. STREET

George runs down street until he comes opposite a two
story building with a sign on it reading, "Bailey
Building and Loan Association." He stops, undecided.
He takes out the package of pills and turns it over
in his hands. His indecision is acute. Suddenly he
decides and crosses street on the run and up a stairway.

INT.   STAIRWAY

There is a large finger painted on the stairway pointing
up the stairs, with a sign on it reading, "Bailey
Building and Loan, 2nd Floor." George starts up the
stairs, two at a time.

INT. OUTER OFFICE, BUILDING AND LOAN - DAY -

FULL SHOT. The offices are ancient and a bit on the
rickety side. There is a counter with grill, somewhat
like a bank. In the outer office the personnel consists
of a waspish woman, seated at a desk pounding a
typewriter, and a clerk behind the grill, busy with
a calculating machine.

                                        (CONTINUED)

Before a door marked: PETER BAILEY, PRIVATE,
George's Uncle Billy stands, obviously trying to
hear what is going on inside. He is a very good-
humored man of about forty, in shirt-sleeves with
black cuff protectors. The importance of the talk
going on in Billy's worried look, the harassed
expression on the face of the lady at the typewriter,
Cousin Tilly Bailey, and the feverishly anxious
expression on the face of the clerk at the calculating
machine, Cousin Eustace Bailey. The office vibrates
with an aura of crisis as George enters and proceeds
directly toward his father's office when Uncle Billy
grabs him by the arm.

                           UNCLE BILLY
                Avast there, Captain Cook!
                Where you headin'?

                           GEORGE
                Got to see Pop, Uncle Billy.

                           UNCLE BILLY
                Some other time, George.

Tilly goes to answer switchboard. Eustace goes to
adding machine.

                           GEORGE
                It's important!

                           UNCLE BILLY
                No, son, no - not now. There's
                a squall in there that's shapin'
                up into a storm.

During the foregoing Cousin Tilly has answered the
telephone on her desk, and now she calls out:

                           COUSIN TILLY
                Uncle Billy - telephone -

                           UNCLE BILLY
                Who is it?

                           COUSIN TILLY
                The Bank examiner.

                           UNCLE BILLY
                Bank examiner? Oh, I should have
                called him yesterday.

Cousin Eustace registers sudden shock.

                           (CONTINUED)

                              UNCLE BILLY (cont'd)
                    (a doomed
                     expression)
          Oh-oh.
                    (shakes his head;
                     to George)
          Did I say storm? I should
          have said typhoon.
                    (to Cousin Tilly)
          Switch it inside.

He walks away to a door marked: WILLIAM BAILEY,
PRIVATE, opens it and enters. George stands irresolute
a moment, aware of crisis in the affairs of the Bailey
Building and Loan Assoication, but aware more keenly
of his father's office and sees:

INT. BAILEY'S PRIVATE OFFICE

MED. SHOT - George's father is seated behind his desk,
nervously drawing swirls on a pad. He looks tired and
worried. He is a gentle man in his forties, an idealist
stubborn only for other people's rights. Nearby, in
his throne-like wheelchair, behind which stands the
goon who furnishes the motive power, sits Potter, his
bald head gleaming, his squarish derby hat in his hand.
The following dialogue is fast and heated, as though
the argument had been in process for some time.

                         POTTER
          Peter Bailey, you've been
          trying to do business in this
          town without me. Against me!
          Now you're crying -

                         BAILEY
          I'm not crying, Mr. Potter.

                         POTTER
          Well, you're begging and that's
          a whole lot worse.

                         BAILEY
          All I'm asking is thirty days more,
          Mr. Potter -- Just thirty short days.

George enters.

                         GEORGE
          Pop! Pop!

                        BAILEY
Just a minutes, son.
        (to Potter)
I'll dig up that five thousand
somehow.

                        POTTER
Have you put any real pressure
on your people to pay their
mortgages?

                        BAILEY
Times are bad -

                        GEORGE
A lot of them are out of work.

                        POTTER
        (shouting)
Then foreclose!

                        BAILEY
        (shouting back)
I can't do that. Those families
have children.

                        GEORGE
Pop!

                        POTTER
They're somebody's children,
Mr. Potter.

                        POTTER
Are you running a business or a
charity ward? Well not with my
money. Look, you need me. I
run the county. And I'll have to
run this Building and Loan. Give
me control or I'll close you up.

                        BAILEY
What makes you such a hard
skulled character? You've no
family - no children - you'll
never spend all the money you've got --

                        POTTER
So I should give it to miserable
failures like you and that idiot
brother of yours to spend for me --

                              (CONTINUED)

                    GEORGE
               (forgetting his
                own troubles)
          He's <u>not</u> a failure! You can't say
          that about my father!

                    BAILEY
               (going toward him)
          George, George --

                    GEORGE

          You're not! You're the biggest
          man in town.

                    BAILEY

          Run along, son.

                    GEORGE

          Bigger'n him - bigger'n
          everybody --

                    POTTER

          Gives you an idea of the Baileys --

                    BAILEY

          Run along, son. I'm very busy
          with Mr. Potter --

                    GEORGE

          Don't let him say things like
          that about you --

                    BAILEY

          Okay son, run along. I'll talk
          to you tonight.

He closes door on George and turns to Potter.   Somehow
his son's visit has stiffened his backbone.

                    POTTER

          If it was me, I'd talk to him
          with a strap. Well, what's the
          answer?

                    BAILEY

          Mr. Potter, you've humiliated me
          in front of my son. I'll tell
          you what the answer is - you can
          take all your money, your wheelchair,
          that stone-faced goon of yours and
          jump into the biggest safe you've got.

                                        (CONTINUED)

                    POTTER
          I see - uh-huh -

CAMERA PULLS BACK TO a shot which includes Joseph and
Clarence.

                    JOSEPH
          George never knew it, but he
          saved his father's business that
          day.

                    CLARENCE
          Yes, but what about the capsules?
          That's what I'm worried about.

                    JOSEPH
          You - and George.

As Clarence bends forward to look at the screen:

INT. OUTER OFFICE, BUILDING & LOAN ASSOCIATION

CLOSE SHOT - George. He had forgotten his trouble
(as he always does) because of somebody else's trouble,
but now his personal problem comes back to him. He
takes the box of capsules out of his pocket and looks at
it. He glances toward the door marked, PETER BAILEY,
realizes this is no time to interrupt his father again,
and starts toward the door marked, WILLIAM BAILEY,
PRIVATE.

INT. UNCLE BILLY'S PRIVATE OFFICE

MED. SHOT - As George pokes his head into the door,
Uncle Billy, at his desk, sweat popping out on his
brow and chewing on a stub of cigar, is speaking on
the phone. His mood is one propitiatory, almost servile
hinge-necking. His head keeps nodding like a bobbin
on a loom.

                    UNCLE BILLY
               (waving George out)
          Yes, yes.

                    GEORGE
          Uncle Billy!

                    UNCLE BILLY
               (on phone)
          Yes, Mr. Purdy...

He gestures violently to George to close the door and
beat it.

                              UNCLE BILLY (cont'd)
          Absolutely... Naturally, Mr.
          Purdy...Of course... Certainly...
          Yes, we'll be ready - We're working
          on that right -

He sees that George is still there and again
pantomimes him to beat it. CAMERA PANS DOWN TO the
wastebasket into which Uncle Billy has thrown the
match.

INT. OUTER OFFICE - AT GRILL COUNTER

CLOSE SHOT - Behind the grill Cousin Eustace is working
at the calculating machine, as George comes INTO SHOT.
With one hand Eustace keeps flipping papers, with the
other he jabs at the keys of the machine. He is
obviously in a state of great nervous tension. His
lips move like Gene Krupa's when he plays the drums.

                              COUSIN TILLY
                 (on phone)
          It's the end this time, Martha -
          it's the end.

                              GEORGE
          Cousin Eustace --

Eustace's left hand goes up like a traffic cop's
halting all traffic, without a letup in the activity
of his jabbing right hand.

                              COUSIN EUSTACE
          Bank examiner!

He concentrates on his St. Vitus dance at the
calculating machine. George realizes it is impossible
to interrupt Cousin Eustace's frantic chore.

INT. OUTER OFFICE

CLOSE SHOT - Cousin Tilly. Cousin Tilly is speaking
on the telephone on her desk, which looks like a
miniature kitchen. A pot of coffee is simmering on
an electric plate; there are some hard-boiled eggs
and pound cake in evidence. Tilly's voice is as
dolorous as her face.

                              COUSIN TILLY
                 (on phone)
          Potter's here and the bank
          examiner's coming. It's the
          day of judgment, Martha.

                                        (CONTINUED)

                              GEORGE
                    Cousin Tilly --

                              COUSIN TILLY
                         (inquiringly)
                    Yes, George?

Before George can speak, the panicky voice of Uncle
Billy bellows from his office:

                              UNCLE BILLY'S VOICE
                    Tilly! Cousin Tilly, quick!

Cousin Tilly sets down the receiver and CAMERA PANS
her over to Uncle Billy's office. She opens the door
and as she rushes in:

INT. UNCLE BILLY'S OFFICE

MED. SHOT - Uncle Billy is still vigorously "yessing"
Mr. Purdy, as Cousin Tilly enters.

                              UNCLE BILLY
                    Positively, Mr.Purdy -

Frantically he gestures toward the wastebasket from
which smoke is billowing. In pantomime, as he
continues "yessing" the bank examiner, he indicates
he expects her to function as fire department.

                              UNCLE BILLY (cont'd)
                    Yes, yes, Mr. Purdy...

Cousin Tilly rushes over to the basked, takes a quick
gander at the fire, hesitates, then rushes out again.

INT. OUTER OFFICE.

FULL SHOT. Cousin Tilly runs out of Uncle Billy's
office, over to her desk, grabs the coffee pot, and
rushes back into Uncle Billy's office.

                              UNCLE BILLY
                         (on phone)
                    That's what I say, Mr. Purdy...

Cousin Tilly rushes over to the wastebasket and
begins pouring coffee into it.

                              UNCLE BILLY (cont'd)
                    Yes, sir...!

                                        (CONTINUED)

CLOSE SHOT - George. Worried and frustrated, he
takes the box of capsules, looks at it and comes to
a decision entirely on his own. CAMERA PANS WITH him
as he starts out of the office.

                                    DISOLVE TO:

INT. GOWER'S STORE - AN HOUR LATER - DAY

INSERT: THE DRUG STORE TELEPHONE RINGING,
               insistently, ominously.

CLOSEUP - Gower. His befuddled face comes up from
his hands.

CLOSE SHOT - At drug store counter. Mary Hatch is
still seated at the counter with her dish of ice
cream. Her anxious eyes are fixed on George, who is
polishing the counter. The SOUND of the phone
ringing causes him to stop his chore. He starts
fearfully in the direction of the phone. Mary looks
after him, open mouthed, with suspense and anxiety.

MED. SHOT - At phone. Gower stumbles across, picking
up receiver. George stands flatly against the wall,
listening apprehensively.

                        GOWER
                 (on phone)
            Yes? Who? Oh, yes, Mrs.
            Blaine. Yes? What!
                 (then)
            You shoulda had that medicine
            an hour ago. You'll have it in
            five minutes, Mrs. Blaine.

He hangs up the phone and looks drunkenly at George.
Then he pushes him roughly into the back room.

INT. DRUGSTORE - PRESCRIPTION ROOM - DAY

Gower stands threateningly over George.

                        GOWER
            Where's Mrs. Blaine's box of
            capsules?
                 (as George is silent)
            Did you hear what I said? What sort
            of tricks are you playing anyway?

                                    (CONTINUED)

He slaps George on his bad ear. The boy winces and
puts his hand to his ear.

                         GOWER (cont'd)
               Why didn't you deliver them
               right away? Don't you know
               that boy's very sick?

                         GEORGE
                    (frantically)
               Yes, sir...I...

Gower has George by his collar and slaps both ears
this time.

                         GEORGE (cont'd)
               You're hurting my sore ear.

INT. DRUG STORE AT COUNTER

CLOSE SHOT - Mary. We hear two more slaps, loud.
Mary winces and recoils as though she herself were
receiving the blows.

INT. PRESCRIPTION ROOM

MED. SHOT. Gower still has George by the collar and
is shaking him fiercely.

                         GOWER
                    (fiercely)
               You lazy loafer! What're you
               trying to do? Ruin me? Sick
               boy and you off reading magazines.
               Stealing and reading magazines.

He hits George twice again. The boy twists out of
his hand and backs up to the wall, knocking down some
bottles.

INT. DRUG STORE AT COUNTER

CLOSE SHOT - Mary. Tears roll down her cheeks as
she hears:

                         GEORGE'S VOICE
                    (terrified despair)
               Mr. Gower, you don't know what
               you're doing. You put something
               wrong in those capsules.

                                        (CONTINUED)

INT. PRESCRIPTION ROOM

CLOSE SHOT - Gower and George.

                    GEORGE
              (his voice
              breaking)
         I know you're unhappy. You got
         that telegram and you're upset.
         You put something bad in those
         capsules and I didn't know what
         to do. It's not your fault, Mr.
         Gower....

George pulls the little box out of his pocket. Gower
savagely rips it away from him, breathing heavily,
staring at the boy venemously.

                    GEORGE (cont'd)
         Just look and see what you did,
         Mr. Gower. Look at the bottle
         you took the powder from. It's
         poison! I tell you it's poison.
         I know you feel bad....and....

George falters off, cupping his aching ear with a hand.
Gower looks at the large brown bottle which has not
been replaced on the shelf. He fears open the package,
shakes some powder out of one capsule, cautiously
tastes it, then abruptly throws the whole mess to the
table and turns to look at George again. The boy is
whimpering, hurt, frightened. Gower steps toward him.

                    GEORGE (cont'd)
         Don't hurt my sore ear again.
         Dont' hurt my ear again.

But this time Gower sweeps the boy to him in a hug
and, sobbing hoarsely, crushes the boy in his embrace.
George is crying, too.

                    GOWER
         Oh, George, George, George....
         Oh, George, George, George....

                    GEORGE
         Mr. Gower, I won't ever tell a
         soul. I know what you're feeling,
         Mr. Gower. I won't ever tell
         anyone....hope to die, I won't!

                    GOWER
              (hoarsely sobbing)
         Oh, George, George, George....
         Oh, George, George, George....

                                        FADE OUT

INT. LUGGAGE SHOP - DAY (1928)

MED. SHOT. It is late afternoon. A young man is
looking over an assortment of luggage. At his side
stands Joe Hepner, the proprietor of the place. The
customer's back is to camera. Under his breath he
is whistling: "As I Was Walking Down The Street."

                    JOE
              (indicating one of
               the pieces of luggage)
          There's the slickest number in the
          shop. An overnight bag, genuine
          Russian Morocco, combination lock,
          fitted up with brushes, combs,
          shaving set --

                    THE CUSTOMER
          Nope.

As CAMERA MOVES UP CLOSER TO him, he turns and we get
our first glimpse of George as a young man. CAMERA
HAS MOVED UP TO a CLOSEUP by now.

                    GEORGE
          Nope. Nope. Nope. Nope. I
          want something big --

Suddenly, in action, the picture freezes and becomes
a still.

INT. PROJECTION ROOM - HEAVEN - DAY

TWO SHOT - Joseph and Clarence.

                    CLARENCE
          What did you stop it for?

                    JOSEPH
          I want you to get a good look
          at that face.

                    CLARENCE
          Who is it?

                    JOSEPH
          George Bailey.

                    CLARENCE
          You mean the kid that had his
          ears slapped back by the druggist?

                              (CONTINUED)

                         JOSEPH
          That's the kid.

                         CLARENCE
          It's a good face. I like him.
          I like George Bailey. I'm
          interested in him.
                   (eagerly)
          Tell me, did he ever tell anyone
          about the pills?

                         JOSEPH
          Not a soul.

                         CLARENCE
          Did he ever marry the girl?
          Did he ever go exploring?

                         JOSEPH
          Well, let's see....

CLOSE SHOT - the screen. The arrested CLOSEUP of
George springs to life again.

                         GEORGE
          I don't want anything for one
          night. I want something for a
          hundred and one. With lots of
          room for labels -- from Egypt,
          Baghdad, Sammarkand....A big
          one, Joe.

                         JOE
                   (taking down a
                    large bag)
          I see, a flying carpet, eh?
          Don't suppose you'd like this
          old broken-down job, would you?

                         GEORGE
          Now you're talking. Boy, I
          could use that as a raft in
          case the boat sunk. How much
          is this one?

                         JOE
          No charge.

                         GEORGE
          How's that?
                   (touching his ear)
          That's my trick ear, Joe. It
          sounded as if you said no charge.

                                        (CONTINUED)

                              JOE
                    That's right.

                              GEORGE
                    But it's got my name on it.

                              JOE
                    A little present from old man
                    Gower. Came down and picked it
                    out himself.

                              GEORGE
                    He did? Whatta you know --
                    my old boss -- whatta you know --

                              JOE
                    Yep. What boat you sailing on?

                              GEORGE
                         (peeling
                          off money)
                    Working across on a cattle boat.

                              JOE
                    A cattle boat?

                              GEORGE
                    Okay -- I like cows.

                              JOE
                    All right, all right. I didn't
                    mean -- Hey! Cows don't get
                    seasick, do they?

                              GEORGE
                         (on his way out)
                    I don't know.
                         (waving)
                    But I'll find out.

EXT. STREET - DAY

The CAMERA FOLLOWS George as he comes out of the shop
and starts along the street, very conscious of his
bag. A man passes him on the street.

                              MAN
                    Leaving? Have a good trip.

                              GEORGE
                    Thanks.

As he goes on, he comes to Gower's drugstore. He
starts in.

INT. GOWER DRUGSTORE - DAY

The place is practically the same except that it is
now full of school kids having sodas, etc. A juke
box and many little tables have been added. It has
become the hangout of the local small fry. There
are now three kids jerking sodas.

Gower is a different man now -- sober, shaven and
good humoured. He is behind counter, waiting on
customers, when George comes in. Gower's face lights
up when he sees George.

FRANK
CAPRA

(
(
(GEORGE
(How are ya, Mr. Gower?
(
(GOWER
(Hello, George.
(
(GEORGE
(Gee, thanks for the bag -- it's
(wonderful of you.
(
(GOWER
(Forget it.
(
(GEORGE
(Just what I wanted -- wonderful.
(
(GOWER
(Hope you enjoy it, George.
(
(GEORGE
((sees cigar lighter)
(Oh oh -- wish I had a million
(dollars.
((strikes lighter)
(Hot dog!
(
(KIDS
((ad lib)
(Hot dog!
(
(GEORGE
((notices fountain)
(Gee whiz -- my old soda fountain!
(Well, ye olde apothecary shoppe
(ain't what she used to be, is it?

(CONTINUED)

                         GOWER
(After school they swarm in here
(like ants. Come over here.
((starts putting
(cigarettes in
(George's pocket)
(So you're leaving? Always knew
(those National Geographics would
(get you.
(
(GEORGE
(Gee -- thanks, Mr. Gower.
(
(GOWER
(How long will you be gone?

                         GEORGE
        Three months. Coming back for
        college in the fall.

                         GOWER
             (surprised)
        College? Thought you gave up
        that idea when you went in with
        your father in the Building and
        Loan?

                         GEORGE
        Nope, nope, nope. Been working
        there the last three years to
        get enough money to see me through
        school, that's all -- Lookit here....
             (pulls out bank
               book and shows
               it to Gower)
        You're the one that started me --
        with that big buck a week you
        used to pay me.

                         GOWER
             (reading the
               bank book)
        Fourteen hundred! George, you
        can get married and have kids
        with that.

                         GEORGE
             (taking back book)
        No-o-ope, nope, nope, nope.

                         GOWER
        George, I'll sell you half
        interest in my place for that!

                                        (CONTINUED)

                              GEORGE
              No-o-ope, nope, nope, nope.

Some of the kids nearby take it up.

                               KIDS
              No-o-ope, nope, nope, nope.

                              GEORGE
                     (good humouredly,
                      turning to kids)
              No-o-ope, nope, nope, nope.

                              GOWER
              George, you aren't thinking of
              leaving Bedford Falls for good?

                              GEORGE
              No-o-ope, nope - Ye-o-ep, yep,
              yep, yep.

                               KIDS
              No-o-ope, nope - nope - nope.

                              GEORGE
              Ye-o-ep, yep, yep, yep.

                              GOWER
                     (getting the spirit)
              No-o-ope, nope, nope, nope.

Potter comes in the door and watches proceedings with
a vinegar face.

                              GEORGE
                     (to Gower)
              Good-by-eee, good-bye, goodbye,
              goodbye.
                     (shakes his hand)

                               KIDS
              Good-bye-ee-e. Goodbye, goodbye,
              goodbye. No-o-ope, nope, nope,
              nope. Ye-e-ep, yep, yep, yep.

Everybody starts shouting their own version. George
waves at them and starts hurriedly out. He runs into
Potter, grabbing his hand, George pumps it up and down.

                              GEORGE
                     (to Potter)
              Good-bye-e-e-e. Goodbye,
              goodbye, goodbye.

                                        (CONTINUED)

                         POTTER
                    (disgusted)
          No wonder the country's going
          to pot.

                         GEORGE
                    (with a knowing
                     look toward kids)
          Well, as long as it doesn't go
          to Potter! Ha, ha!

A shriek of laughter from the kids, as George runs
out. Gower laughs explosively, but laugh freezes
on his face as he catches Potter's vinegar look.

George crossing street whistling his pet tune. He
spots Ernie and his cab, and Bert the motor cop,
parked alongside.

                         GEORGE
          Hey, Ernie!
Ernie holds door open for him.

                         ERNIE
          Hiya, George.

                         GEORGE
          Hi, Ernie - Hi, Bert.

                         BERT
          Hiyah, fella.

                         GEORGE
          Ernie, I'm a rich tourist today.
          Ride me home in style.

                         ERNIE
          Hop in your highness, hop in. I'll put
          on my cap for the carriage trade.

As George has door open, he stops suddenly as he sees
Violet, (now obviously a little sex machine) come
toward him. Her walk and figure would stop anybody.
She gives him a sultry look.

                         VIOLET
          Good evening, Mr. Bailey.

(CONTINUED)

                        GEORGE
            Hello Violet. You look swell --
            some dress you got on.

                        VIOLET
            Oh, this old thing. I only put
            it on when I don't care how I look.

All three men follow her with their eyes as she walks
away. George sees the other two still intently looking.
George and Bert stand on running board to follow Violet
with their eyes.

                        ERNIE
            George, how would you like --

                        GEORGE
            Yes....
                (gets in cab)

Ernie roars. He leans out to Bert, the cop.

                        ERNIE
                (to Bert)
            Bert -- ride with us? Show you
            the town.

                        BERT
                (looking at watch)
            No -- think I'll go home and
            see what the wife's doing.

                        ERNIE
                (indicating Bert)
            Family man.

INT. CAB - PROCESS

George, holding Uncle Billy's bird on his arm, sits
in the back seat of Ernie's cab. Ernie is driving.

                        GEORGE
            Put the flag down, you dope --
            you're losing money.

                        ERNIE
            No - this is on the house for
            the plug you put in for me at the
            Building and Loan.

                                            (CONTINUED)

                              GEORGE
                       (overlapping Ernie's
                        line - out window)
                 Hi, Charlie! -- Tomorrow.

                              ERNIE
                 The wife wanted me to thank you --
                       (George starts to
                        sing Buffalo Gal)
                 After all, you designed the house,
                 floated the loan and practically
                 built the house.

George pauses long enough in his singing to yell
outside window.

                              GEORGE
                 Hi! Bill - Yeah...
                       (he continues
                        singing, drowning
                        out Ernie)

                              ERNIE
                 Oh, all right, all right....
                       (and he too joins
                        in singing Buffalo
                        Gal)

                                        DISSOLVE OUT

DISSOLVE IN

INT. DOWNSTAIRS - DINNING ROOM

Pop Bailey is about to sit down to dinner. Mother
Bailey and Annie, the cook, look up toward vibrating
ceiling. There are SOUNDS of terrific banging and
scuffling.

                              MOTHER
                 George! Harry! You're shaking
                 the house down! Stop it!

                              POP
                 Let 'em alone - wish I was up
                 there with 'em.

                                        (CONTINUED)

                         MOTHER
          Harry'll tear his dinner suit!
          George!

                         ANNIE
          That's why all children should
          be girls.

Mother starts upstairs.

                         MOTHER
               (going upstairs)
          George! Harry! Come down to
          dinner this minute. You know
          we've been waiting for you --
          everything's getting cold!

INT. DOWNSTAIRS - DINING ROOM

Pop is smiling and poking his plate. Annie is banging
the ceiling with the end of a broom. A commotion is
heard on the stairs, the boys imitating fan-fare MUSIC.
Down they come holding ma between them high up on their
hands. They bring her into dining room and deposit
her gracefully into Pop's lap.

                         GEORGE
          Here, Pop - got a present for you.

Pop kisses her hand gallantly, after wiping his
mustache. The boys applaud vigorously shouting "Bravo!
Bravo!" Mother gives Pop a quick hug, then turns with
all the wrath she can assume on the two boys.

                         MOTHER
          You idiots! Sit down, George
          and have your dinner.

                         GEORGE & HARRY
               (ad lib)
          Yes M'am. Yes, M'am.

                         HARRY
          I've eaten.

                         MOTHER
          Harry, are you gonna dress for
          your graduation party or not?
          Look at you!

                                          (CONTINUED)

                         HARRY
          It's George's tux, I don't care.
          Annie, sweetheart, have you got
          those pies.

He tries to embrace her.

                         ANNIE
          If you lay a hand on me, I'll
          hit you with this broom.

                         HARRY
          Annie, I'm in love with you --
          there's a moon out tonight.

As he pushes her through the kitchen door, he slaps
her fanny. She screams. The noise is shut off by
the swinging door. George sits down to eat.

                         GEORGE
          Boy, boy, boy - my last meal
          at the Bailey Boarding House.

                         MOTHER
                (fanning herself)
          My lands, my blood pressure!

                         HARRY
                (coming out)
          Pop, can I have the car? I have
          to take over a lot of plates and
          things.

                         MOTHER
                (jumping up)
          What plates?

                         HARRY
          Mom - I'm Chairman of the Eats
          Committee. We only need a
          couple of dozen!

                         MOTHER
          No you don't, now, Harry. Not
          my best Haviland - not my best
          Haviland!

                         GEORGE
          Oh, give him the plates, Ma --
          give him the plates.

                                        (CONTINUED)

She follows Harry into kitchen, leaving Pop and
George. There is a great similarity and a great
understanding between them.

> POP
>
> Hope you have a nice trip, George.
> Uncle Billy and I are going to
> miss you.

> GEORGE
>
> I'm going to miss you, too.
> What's the matter, Pop, you
> look tired?

> POP
>
> Had another tussle with Potter
> today. I thought when we put
> him on the Board of Directors,
> he'd ease up on us a little bit.

> GEORGE
>
> What's eating that old money-
> grubbing buzzard anyway?

> POP
>
> Sick man, son. He's frustrated.
> Sick in his mind, sick in his
> soul, if he had one. Hates
> everybody that has things he can't
> have.
> > (with a little
> > laugh)
> Hates us mostly, I guess.

Harry and Mother come out of kitchen, Harry carrying
plates and pies.

> MOTHER
>
> You take that stuff to the car.
> Hurry up. I'll get your tie
> and studs together.

> HARRY
>
> So long, Pop -- Gangway, Gangway!
> You coming later, George?

> GEORGE
>
> What, and be bored to death?

> HARRY
>
> Couldn't want a better death. Lots
> of pretty girls -- and by the way,
> George, we're going to use that new
> floor tonight.

                        GEORGE
        Hope it works.

                        POP
        No gin tonight, son!

                        HARRY
                    (over his shoulder)
        Aw, just a little, Pop.

                        POP
        No sir, not a drop.

Harry and Mother go out.

                        ANNIE
                    (at kitchen door)
        Boys and girls and music - why
        do they need gin?

She goes back to kitechen.

                        GEORGE
        Did I act like that when I
        graduated from high school?

                        POP
        Pretty much. Wish we could send
        Harry to college with you, George.
        Your mother and I talked it over
        half the night.

                        GEORGE
        We got it all figured out, Pop.
        Harry'll take my job at the
        Building and Loan, work there
        four years, then he'll go.

                        POP
        He's pretty young for that job.

                        GEORGE
        No younger than I was.

                        POP
        Well, you were born older, George.

                        GEORGE
        How's that?

                        POP
        I said you were born older. I
        suppose you've decided, son, what
        you're going to do when you get out
        of college.

                                    (CONTINUED)

                         GEORGE
              Well, you know what I've been
              talking about - build things -
              design new buildings --

Annie comes in again.

                         GEORGE (cont'd)
              ---plan modern cities -- well,
              you know ---

                         POP
              Still after that first million
              before you're thirty.

                         GEORGE
              I'll settle for half in cash, Pop.

                         POP
              Just a hope of course, son - but
              you wouldn't consider coming back
              to the Building and Loan, would
              you?

Annie stops to hear answer.

                         GEORGE
                    (to Annie)
              Annie, why don't you sit down?
              Be more comfortable and you
              could hear better.

                         ANNIE
              I would if I thought you'd say
              anything worth listening to.

                         GEORGE
              You would, eh?

She gives George a look, and goes on out to the kitchen.
Bailey smiles and turns to George.

                         POP
              I know it's soon to talk about it.

                         GEORGE
              Gee, Pop, I couldn't. I couldn't
              face cooped up the rest of my
              life in a shabby little office...
                    (then as he realized he
                     may have hurt his father's
                     feelings)

                                        (CONTINUED)

                          GEORGE (cont'd)
          Sorry - I didn't mean...but this
          business of nickels and dimes....
          spending your life trying to figure
          out how to save three cents on a
          length of pipe...I'd go crazy. I
          want something big... something
          important.

                          POP
               (quietly)
          You know, George, I feel that in
          our small way we're doing
          something important. It's
          satisfying a fundamental urge -
          It's deep in the human race - for
          a man to want his own roof and
          walls and fireplace. We help him
          get those in our shabby little
          office.

                          GEORGE
               (unhappily)
          I know, Pop. I wish I -- but
          I've been hoarding pennies like
          a miser in order to...Most of
          my friends have already finished
          college - Pop, I just feel as if
          I had to get away or I'd bust.

                          POP
          Son, yeah, yeah. You're right.

                          GEORGE
          You know what I mean...

                          POP
          This town's no place for anybody
          unless you crawl to Potter.
          You've got talent, son. I've
          seen it. Get yourself an
          education. Then get out.

                          GEORGE
          Pop, you want a shock? I think
          you're a pretty great guy.

To cover his embarrassment, he cups his hands like a
megaphone and directs his voice to kitchen.

                          GEORGE (cont'd)
          Hear that, Annie?

                                              (CONTINUED)

                         ANNIE'S VOICE
              I heard it. About time one of
              you lunkheads said it.

                         GEORGE
                    (to his father)
              I'm going to miss old Annie.
              Pop. I think I'll get dressed
              and go over to Harry's party.

                         POP
              Have a good time, son.

George goes.

                         MOTHER
                    (comes in)
              Oh those boys, those boys. How
              do you feel, Peter?

                         FATHER
              I never felt better in my life.
              George just said I was a great
              guy.

                         MOTHER
                    (kises his brow)
              That's not news to me.

                                        DISSOLVE

EXT. HIGH SCHOOL PAVILION - NIGHT

In the center is a beautifully lighted fountain which
tumbles into a good-sized pool at its base. The
dancers dance around the fountain. At the other end
is a long table with punch bowl, glasses, and sandwiches.
The dance pavilion is enclosed by arbors and gardens.
Behind the orchestra is a big banner reads:

                 BEDFORD FALLS HIGH SCHOOL
                     CLASS OF 1928

Abouit fifty or sixty young couples are dancing to
the prevailing fox trot of the year 1928.

George and Harry, with their arms piled high with
plates, come into the entrance.

CLOSER SHOT - Harry and George. Just as they come in,
the dance finishes. The couples break...the girls
huddling together around the punch bowl. Harry yells
to the boys.

                                        (CONTINUED)

                             HARRY
           Hi there. Give a hand.

Several of the boys come up to him, taking the plates
from his hands, and from George. George looks at them,
feeling very grown-up and out of place.

                             BOYS
                    (ad lib)
           You're late.
           'Lo Harry.
           Give 'em to me.
           You ought to try the floor.
           It's neat, etc.

One of the boys takes the plates from George.

                             HARRY
                    (introducing George)
           You know my kid brother? I'm
           going to put him through college.

                             BOYS
           Hi. Hello there.

                             SAM'S VOICE
           George.

George swings around, delighted to hear a familiar
voice.

WIDER ANGLE - including Sam Wainwright and Marty Hatch.
Sam is coming toward George. He is assured and breezy,
wearing very collegiate clothes. He greets George
with his familiar gesture.

                             SAM
           Hee-haw! Hee-haw!

                             GEORGE
           Oh-oh, Sam Wainwright! When did
           you get back?

                             SAM
           This afternoon. Thought I'd
           give the kids a treat.

                             GEORGE
           Old college graduate now, huh?

                                            (CONTINUED)

                          SAM
         Yep. Old Joe college Wainwright.
         Hee-haw!
              (slaps George
               on back)
         Well, freshman, looks like you're
         going to make it at last, huh?

                          GEORGE
         Yep. I'll have a beard down
         to here before I ---

Sam sees Harry and leaves George in the middle of a
gesture.

                          SAM
              (to Harry)
         Harry! -- you're the guy I want
         to see. Coach has heard all
         about you.

                          HARRY
         He has?

                          SAM
         Sure! Followed all your games --
         his mouth's watering. He wants
         me to find out if you're going
         to come along with us.

                          HARRY
              (sadly)
         Well, I gotta make some dough
         first.

                          SAM
         Make it fast. We need great
         ends like you --
              (slapping George
               on shoulder)
         --not broken down old guys like
         this! Hee-haw!
              (hands to ears)

                          GEORGE
              (hands to ears)
         Hee-haw!

An elderly, fussy school principal comes over to George.

                                    (CONTINUED)

                    PRINCIPAL
              (shaking hands)
     George, welcome back. Putting
     a pool under this floor was a
     great idea. Saved us another
     building. Harry, Sam, having
     a lot of fun! Cut yourself a
     piece of cake - lot of pretty
     girls around --

                    GEORGE
     Thanks, Mr. Partridge.

                    FREDDIE
     I was in the 2nd lane. I came
     up to 3rd place and the first
     thing I knew, one of the guys
     tripped me and I guess that's why
     I came out in 4th place - it
     would have been a cinch if it
     hadn't been for him, etc., etc.

Violet suddenly barges in with a program.

                    VIOLET
     Got a third of a dance left -
     a third of a dance. What am I
     bid!

                    SAM
     Vi! -- Look who's here!

                    MARTY
              (taking
               George's arm)
     George...

                    GEORGE
     H'yer, Marty. Well, it's old
     home week.

                    MARTY
     Do me a favor, will you? You
     remember my kid sister, Mary.

                    SAM
              (imitating Mary)
     "Momma wants you, Marty."

                    MARTY
     Dance with her, will you?

                              (CONTINUED)

                         GEORGE
          Me? I feel funny enough already,
          with all these kids.

                         MARTY
               (easing him along
                toward the punch
                bowl)
          Come on. Be a sport. Just dance
          her around one time and you'll
          give her the thrill of her life.
               (calling off)
          Hey, sis.

                         GEORGE
               (to Violet)
          Well, excuse me, Violet.
               (back to Marty)
          Don't you take long now. I don't
          want to be a wet nurse for...

He stops suddenly as he sees Mary, staring at her.
Violet turns to Sam.

                         SAM
               (to her)
          Vi - look who's here!

                         VIOLET
          Sam!

They dance off.

WIDER ANGLE - including Mary Hatch and Freddie. She
is standing talking to one of the boys (Freddie) a
glass of punch in her hand. For the first time she
is wearing an evening gown and she has gained assurance
from the admiration of the boy with her. She turns
around and for the first time she sees George. For a
second she loses her poise, staring at him. Freddie
continues talking (ad lib):

                         MARTY
          You remember George? This is
          Mary. Well, I'll be seeing you.

He goes off hurriedly, leaving them staring at each
other. George is unable to believe his eyes. She
looks at him shyly, almost overcome with her good
luck. Someone blows a devastating note on the horn.
The MUSIC starts. Freddie comes quickly to Mary.

                                    (CONTINUED)

                      FREDDIE
          Hey, this is my dance.

                      GEORGE
          Why don't you stop annoying
          people.

                      FREDDIE
          I'm sorry...
               (gets it)
          Hey!

George takes Mary in his arms, starting to dance her
away. Freddie stands for a second, looking off after
them.

                      MARY
               (breathlessly)
          Hello.

                      GEORGE
          Hello.

Without looking at Freddie, Mary holds her punch glass
out to him. He takes it, and goes out of the SHOT
with it, eyeing George hostilely.

                      MARY
          You look at me as if you didn't
          know me.

                      GEORGE
          I don't.

                      MARY
          You've passed me on the street
          almost every day.

                      GEORGE
          That was a little girl named
          Mary Hatch. That wasn't you.

MOVING SHOT - Mary and George. Mary dances with George
in a happy daze. He looks down at her appreciatively.
The floor begins to fill up.

Harry is standing in front of orchestra, whistle in
hand.

                      HARRY
               (imitating
                spieler's voice)
          Oyez - oyez - oyez! The big
          Charleston contest!

Cheers go up from crowd.

                    GEORGE
               (looking at Mary
                dubiously)
          Oh, oh.

                    HARRY
          The prize?
               (he holds up small
                statue of adagio couple-
                man holding woman
                up in the air)
          A genoo-ine loving cup! Those
          not tapped by the judges will
          remain on the floor. Let's go!

With a bang, MUSIC goes into a fast Charleston.
Couples begin doing their stuff with the perspiring
abandon of youth.

                    GEORGE
               (smiling at Mary)
          I'm not very good.

                    MARY
               (laughing)
          Neither am I.

                    GEORGE
               (grabbing her)
          Okay -- what can we lose?

Much to their surprise they're pretty good.

                    GEORGE (cont'd)
          Say, you're wonderful!

                    MARY
               (eagerly)
          Let's win it, George.

                    GEORGE
          Okay!

They go to work in earnest. George gets ideas for
steps by watching others. Judges walk around
eliminating couples. Crowds on sidelines cheer for
favorite couples. One couple seems to be getting
plenty of cheers -- Violet and Sam. The competition
is terrific. About thirty couples Charleston their
heads off around the fountain.

                                        (CONTINUED)

CLOSE SHOT - gym wall. Freddie, the kid that lost
a dance with Mary is looking daggers at George. Micky,
a young punk who has had one too many, sidles up to
Freddie.

                    MICKY
          What's the matter, Othello,
          jealous? Sore huh? Did you
          know there's a swimming pool under
          this floor?

Freddie reacts to this.

                    MICKY (cont'd)
          And did you know that button
          behind you causes the floor to
          open up?

Freddie looks.

INSTERT - of control button on switch.

BACK TO SCENE

                    MICKY
          And did you further know that
          I've got the key?

Freddie needs no more. The two boys back up to switch.

INSERT - Freddie's hand pushing button or closing switch.

Floor begins to part in middle, each half sliding
underneath bleacher seats. Pandemonium starts.
Orchestra which has been sitting on floor with back
to wall, begin to be pushed forward as floor moves
out from under them. Dancers begin to scream and try
to get off. Some are so engrossed in dancing they
continue at top speed. Teachers and elders start to
scurry off. As the floor opens, it reveals an
attractive, brilliantly lighted swimming pool.

                    MARY
          They're cheering us.

                    GEORGE
          We must be good.

                                        (CONTINUED)

George and Mary are so busy dancing they don't
notice floor. Spotlights concentrate on them. They
mistake the screams for cheers. They whirl to the
edge of the opening in the floor and fall in. Others
follow them in - some being pushed - some, getting
the spirit, jump in. At top of the excitement -

                                        FADE OUT

FADE IN

EXT. TREE-LINED RESIDENTIAL STREET - NIGHT - CLOSE
(MOVING) SHOT - GEORGE AND MARY

The night is warm with a bright moon. George and
Mary are walking home. George is dressed in jersey
sweater and over-sized football pants, and Mary, in
a much too large robe of the type used on the field
by football players, which trails after her as she
walks. What she has on underneath the robe we do not
know and it's nobody's business. They are singing
"Buffalo Gal" and when they come to the end of a
chorus they exchange a look.

                    GEORGE
          And I told Harry I thought I was
          going to be bored to death! Boy -
          you should have seen the scramble
          in the locker room - I had to knock
          down three people to get these things.

                    MARY
          Do I look as funny as you do?

                    GEORGE
          I guess I'm not the football type.
               (gives her a
               critical survey)
          If it wasn't me talking I'd say
          you were the prettiest girl in
          town. You look wonderful.

                    MARY
          Why don't you say it?

                    GEORGE
          Me! Well, maybe I will say it.
          What happened to you? I mean how'd
          you grow up so --

                    MARY
          I'm catching up with you, George. I
          hope we'll be in the same class at
          College.

                                        (CONTINUED)

                         GEORGE
          Huh? How old are you now?

                         MARY
          Eighteen.

                         GEORGE
          Eighteen -- can you beat that!
          Why, it was only last year that
          you were seventeen.

                         MARY
          Too old or too young?

                         GEORGE
          No, just right. I mean, your age
          fits you. You look a little older
          without your clothes on -- I mean,
          without a dress -- you look a
          little younger -- I mean older --
          I mean --

He steps on the edge of the robe and Mary grabs
frantically to keep it from slipping off, but not
before it has revealed a flash of her bare shoulder.
She readjusts the robe quickly.

                         MARY
                    (exaggerated
                     dignity)
          Please, my train, sir!

                         GEORGE
          A pox upon me for a clumsy lout.

He picks up the end of the robe that he has stepped
on and tenders it to her with flamboyant gesture.

                         GEORGE
          Your caboose, my lady.

                         MARY
          You may kiss my hand.

With a jackknife bow he effects the most cavalier of
hand kissings. For a moment they regard each other.
The moonlight has sifted into their hearts and is
coming out of their ears. Suddenly he bends down and
picks up a rock.

                         GEORGE
          Say, Mary --

ANOTHER ANGLE -

Taking in a weather-beaten, old fashioned two-storied
house in a very rundown state, but showing evidence
of a one-time resplendence.

>   GEORGE
>   I'm going to bust a window of the
>   old Granville house.

>   MARY
>   Oh, no, don't! It's full of
>   romance that old place.

>   GEORGE
>   Why everybody makes a wish and
>   then breaks some glass in it.
>   Got to be a good shot now-a-days.

>   MARY
>   No, George. I love that old
>   place - I'd like to live in it
>   some day.

>   GEORGE
>   I wouldn't live in it as a ghost.

He throws the rock. We hear the SOUND OF broken glass.

>   MARY
>   What's your wish?

>   GEORGE
>   I don't have to make a wish. I
>   know what I'm going to do today,
>   tomorrow and next year and the
>   year after that -- I'm shaking the
>   dust of this crummy little town
>   off my feet. I'm going to see the
>   world - Italy - Greece - the
>   Parthenon - the Coloseum. I'm
>   going to college and see how much
>   they know -- and then I'm going
>   to build things -- air fields --
>   skyscrapers a hundred stories
>   high -- bridges a mile long - and
>   some day I'm going to --

He looks at her and becomes inarticulate. Whatever
his last wish is he can't find words for it. Mary
looks around, sees another stone in the road and picks
it up.   She throws it toward the house and again we
hear the SOUND of breaking glass. George tries to
make his voice casual, but doesn't succeed too well.

                                        (CONTINUED)

                         GEORGE
               Mary, what's your wish?

But Mary's is a secret wish too, and instead of
answering she starts away, singing "Buffalo Gal."
He falls into step beside her.

CLOSE (MOVING) SHOT - MARY AND GEORGE

He joins her in song. When they reach the line: "And
dance by the light of the moon," George continues
changing the rhythm of the song:

                         GEORGE
               Look at the moon; Fine fat old
               moon! And a lunar rainbow!
                    (then resuming
                     conversational tone)
               Sister, tonight I've got hold of
               both ends of the rainbow!
                    (lifts both hands for
                     illustration)
               Oh, boy, I feel like there was
               nothing beyond my reach tonight!
               Just a question of making up your
               mind and then getting it, that's all.

                         MARY
                    (almost inaudibly)
               I know what I want.

                         GEORGE
               You do? Then all you have to do
               is go out and get it.
                    (fiercely)
               Don't let anyone stand in your way.
               Be ruthless -- be cruel, even. What
               is it you want, Mary?

                         MARY
               If I told you it might not come
               true.

                         GEORGE
               That's supersitition, like knocking
               on wood so the avenging gods won't
               hear what you say. There's no
               avenging god - only me. What is it
               you want? The moon? Just say the
               word and I'll throw a lasso around
               it and pull it down for you.

                                        (CONTINUED)

                         MARY
          With one hand, I hope.

                         GEORGE
          With one hand. Just say the word
          and I'll get it with one try.

                         MARY
          I've got the moon. Now what'll
          I do with it?

                         GEORGE
          Swallow it. Then it'll dissolve
          and moonbeams'll shoot out of your
          fingers and your toes and the ends
          of your hair. Am I talking too
          much?

                         OLD MAN
               (a gruff voice o.s.)
          Yes! Why don't you kiss her
          instead of talking her to death?

                         GEORGE
          How's that?

                         OLD MAN
          Why don't you kiss her instead
          of talking her too death?

                         GEORGE
          Kiss her, huh?

They are in front of a house in which a grumpy,
bald-headed old man in shirt sleeves' sits in a rocking
chair on the porch. He gets up off chair and starts
for his door.

                         OLD MAN
          Youth is wasted on the wrong people!

He exits into house, slamming door.

CLOSE SHOT - GEORGE

Mary is OUT OF SHOT but we can see that George's foot
is on the train of her robe again. George is looking
toward the house.

                                         (CONTINUED)

                                GEORGE
                        (truculently)
                Come on out and I'll show you some
                kissing that'll make your hair grow
                back!

O.s., Mary apparently doesn't approve of this notion
of publication osculation and she starts away. The
robe upon which George's foot is firmly planted falls
to the ground. We hear a tiny scream of distress
and then as George turns:

ANOTHER ANGLE

As George looks around Mary is nowhere to be seen.
It seems like moonlight magic. She has disappeard
utterly. He stares about, dubmfounded, then reacts to:

CLOSE SHOT - A HYDRANGEA BUSH - From a slight movement
we can see that Mary has sought refuge behind it.

CLOSE SHOT - GEORGE

He senses Mary's predicament and decides to take some
mischievous advantage. CAMERA MOVES with him as he
starts down the street, singing "Buffalo Gal" and
swinging the robe. As he passes the hydrangea bush:

                                MARY'S VOICE
                Geroge!

George stops and looks around, pretending to be
surprised by the sound of her voice.

                                GEORGE
                Okay - I give up. Where are you?

                                MARY'S VOICE
                Over here, behind the hydrangeas!

                                GEORGE
                Which hydrangeas?

                                MARY'S VOICE
                These!

This is a very interesting situation. One of the
hydrangea bushes shakes violently. George comes over.

                                        (CONTINUED)

CLOSE SHOT - HYDRANGEA BUSH - As George looks at it --

                    GEORGE
          Okay, I give up -- where are you?

                    MARY
          Over here, behind the hydrangea bush.

                    GEORGE
               (starts to toss her the robe)
          Oh, here catch --
               (sizing up the situation)
          Wait a minute...What am I doing?
          This is a very interesting situation.

                    MARY
          Give me my robe, please.

                    GEORGE
               (ignoring her)
          Let's think this thing out....
          A man doesn't get into a situation like
          this every day...
                    MARY
               (interrupting)
          George, I would like my robe...

                    GEORGE
               (not noticing)
          ....Especially in Bedford Falls.
          I've read about things like this,
          but I never came face to face with it.

                    MARY
          George Bailey! Give me my robe right now!
          I'll tell your mother on you!

                    GEORGE
          Oh, she lives way up the street.

                    MARY
          Then I'll call the police.

                    GEORGE
          They're way uptown -- and besides, they'd
          be on my side.

                    MARY
               (screaming)
          I'll scre-A-M!

                                        (CONTINUED)

                              GEORGE
               Maybe I could sell tickets --
               No, the thing is -- I have it!
               I'll make a deal with you, Mary.

                              MARY
               What is it?

Suddenly a car's headlights flash into the scene.
We hear the sound of brakes and Uncle Billy's
voice.

                    UNCLE BILLY'S VOICE
          George!

George turns quickly and looks offscene toward:

CLOSE SHOT AT CURB

Harry has driven up in his little rattletrap of a
car. Uncle Billy is seated next to him. The
expression on their faces plainly indicates they are
bearers of ill tidings.

                              UNCLE BILLY
                    (calls out)
               Come on home, George - quick -
               your father's had a stroke!

CLOSE SHOT - GEORGE

He stands an instant, stricken, then turns.

                              GEORGE
               Here, Mary.

He throws the robe onto the bush and CAMERA PANS
him over to the car.

                              UNCLE BILLY
               Now don't get excited, we've got the doctor.

                              HARRY
               Hop in, George, quick.

As George gets into the car:

CLOSE SHOT - AT HYDRANGEA BUSH

Mary has gotten into the robe and stands looking off,
as offscene we hear the car drive away. Her face is
eloquent of sympathy and concern, as we

                              FADE OUT

INT. BUILDING AND LOAN - DIRECTORS' MEETING - DAY

There are about twelve directors seated around a
long table. They are the substantial citizens of
Bedford Falls: Doctor Campbell, a lawyer, an
insurance agent, a real estate salesman, etc.
Prominently seated among them is Herbert Potter.
The Chairman of the Board of Directors is Doctor
Campbell. Uncle Billy and George are seated among
the directors, near Doctor Campbell. They have
folders and papers before them, on which they have
been reporting. Before each of the directors there
are individual reports for them to study.

                    DR. CAMPBELL
          You've heard all the details --
          all in favor of approving the last loans
          made by the deceased president signify by
          saying "Aye."

                    BOARD
               (all but one)
          Aye!

                    CAMPBELL
          Opposed?

                    POTTER
          No!

                    CAMPBELL
          Motion carried. Loans approved.
               (to George)
          Think that's all we'll need you for, George.
          I know you're anxious to make a train.

                    GEORGE
          Yes, sir, got a taxi waiting downstairs.

                    CAMPBELL
          I'd like the board to know that George gave
          up his trip to Europe just to help
          straighten things out here, this past few
          months. Good luck to you at school, George.

                    GEORGE
               (rising)
          Thanks.

Board members ad lib: Good luck! So long!

                                        (CONTINUED)

                          CAMPBELL
                     (to Board)
          Now we come to the <u>real</u> purpose of this
          meeting --

George nudges Uncle Billy and winks at him knowingly.

                          POTTER
          Mr. Chairman, I want to get to <u>my</u> real
          purpose.

                          MAN
          Now wait a minute, Potter.

                          POTTER
          Wait for what? I claim that this
          institution is not needed in this
          town. It competes with the bank,
          is a general menace to sound
          business practices. Therefore,
          Mr. Chairman, I make a motion that
          this institution be dissolved and
          its assets and liabilities be
          turned over to a receiver --

                          UNCLE BILLY
                     (unable to contain
                      himself, jumps to
                      his feet)
          Potter, you dirty, contemptible --

The chairman pounds his gavel. Others grab Uncle
Billy and restrain him. George looks on, apparently
unmoved.

                          CHAIRMAN
          Order! Billy --

                          UNCLE BILLY
          I'll wring his neck, so help
          me -- George, you hear what
          that buzzard --

                          LAWYER
          Mr. Chairman - it's too soon
          after Peter Bailey's passing to
          discuss chloroforming the
          Building and Loan --

                          ANOTHER MAN
          Peter Bailey died three months
          ago. I second Mr. Potter's motion.

                                        (CONTINUED)

                        CHAIRMAN
          Very well --
               (to George and Billy)
          In that case I'm going to ask
          the two executive officers to
          withdraw. But before you go
          I'm sure the whole Board wishes
          to express its deep sorrow at
          Peter Bailey's passing. It was
          his faith and devotion that are
          responsible for this organization.

                        POTTER
          I'll go further than that --
          I'll say that to the public --
          Peter Bailey <u>was</u> the Building and Loan.

Everyone looks at him surprised.

                        UNCLE BILLY
               (trying to
                control himself)
          Well, Potter, that's fine, coming
          from you -- considering you're the one
          that probably drove him to an early
          grave.

George's face tightens as he tries to lead Uncle
Billy out.

                        POTTER
          Peter Bailey was not a <u>business</u> man --
          <u>that's</u> what killed him. I mean no disrespect
          for him, God rest his soul. He was a
          man of high ideals, so-called. But ideals
          without common sense can <u>ruin</u> this town.
          It isn't fair to the little people to
          encourage them to live beyond their means.
          If they want better homes to live in,
          let 'em wait and save their money. Let
          'em put up a hundred, and we'll lend 'em
          fifty. But here they put up a hunderd and
          borrow a <u>thousand</u>!
               (picking up a
                report from table)
          Take this loan to Ernie Bishop who
          sits on his backside in that taxi
          all day. I happen to know the bank
          turned him down. And here we're
          building him a three thousand dollar
          house! Why?

                                            (CONTINUED)

                        GEORGE
I handled that, sir. You have
all the papers there -- his income
-- his insurance. I can personally
vouch for his character.

                        POTTER
              (sarcastically)
Oh, I see - a personal matter -
He's a friend of yours.
              (turning to others)
That gives you an idea, gentlemen --
if you shoot pool with one of the
employees here, you can borrow
money. And what's that getting us?
A discontented, lazy rabble on our
hands instead of a thrifty working
class. And all because a few
starry-eyed dreamers like Peter
Bailey stir them up and put impossible
ideas in their heads. I say --

                        GEORGE
Just a minute, Mr. Potter. You're <u>right</u>
when you say my father was no <u>business</u>
man. Why he ever started this cheap penny-
ante Building and Loan I'll <u>never</u> know.
But neither you nor anybody else can say
anything against his character, because
his whole life was....
In the twenty-five years since he and
Uncle Billy started this thing he never
once thought of himself. He didn't save
enough money to send <u>Harry</u> to school, let
alone me. But he <u>did</u> help a few people
get out of your slums, Mr. Potter. And
what's wrong with that? What's wrong with
people having a couple of decent rooms and
a bathroom inside instead of those little
outside beauties you provide them with?
Don't they make better citizens? You are
all businessmen. Don't they make better
customers?
              (to Potter)
You say they should save their money and
<u>wait</u> before they think of a decent house.
Wait? For what? Until their children have
grown up and left them? Until they're so
old and beaten they -- Do you know how long
it takes a working man to save five thousand
dollars? People like Ernie Bishop need
their homes <u>now</u>, when their children
are little -- <u>now</u> when they can live with some
dignity by their own fire and under their
own roof. Just remember, Mr. Potter,

                         GEORGE (cont'd)
          that this rabble, as you call them, do
          most of the working, most of the paying,
          most of the living and most of the dying
          in this community. Is it too much for
          them to work and pay, and live and die in
          a couple of clean rooms and a bath? Anyway,
          my father didn't think so. People were
          human beings to him. To you, a warped,
          frustrated old man, they're cattle. In
          my book, Mr. Potter, he died a much richer
          man than you'll ever be!

                         POTTER
          Your book doesn't interest me --
          we're talking about the Building and Loan.

                         GEORGE
          Yes I know what you're talking about,
          Mr. Potter. You're talking about something
          you haven't been able to get your greedy
          fingers into and it's galling you. That's
          what you're talking about -- well, I'm
          talking too much -- I'll get out of....
                 (to Board)
          Gentlemen, you're the Board --
          do what you want. But this town needs
          this measly one-horse institution if only
          to have one place where people can come
          to without crawling to Mr. Potter.
          Come on Uncle Billy -- get your papers
          and let's get out of here.

George leaves the room, followed by the jubilant
Uncle Billy. Potter's face is grim with hatred.

                         POTTER
          Sentimental hogwash! Now -- I want some
          action on my motion --

                         BOARD MEMBERS
                 (all talking at once)
          Just a minute, Potter -- Let me get a
          word in here.
                 (etc.)

INT. OUTSIDE OFFICE

Eustice and Tilly have been eavesdropping at door.
Uncle Billy's crow is in room. George, visibly shaken,
is busy with his bag, his papers. He is worried about
the outcome of the meeting. Dissolving the Building
and Loan will alter all his plans. Uncle Billy follows
him around, chattering.

                    UNCLE BILLY
Boy, oh boy, George, that was telling him,
old boy. You shut his big mouth.

                     EUSTICE
What happened? We heard a lot of yelling.

                    UNCLE BILLY
Well, they're probably voting us out of
business -- after twenty-five years. Well,
easy come easy go!

                      TILLY
          (pacing up and down room with
           newspaper)
Help wanted - Female...here it is.

                    UNCLE BILLY
I don't know what'll happen to us now --
and your mother, poor thing -- and no job
for Henry -- But I don't care, George --
that was worth it -- that was worth it.

Ernie sticks head in doorway.

                      ERNIE
Still want me to wait, George?

                     GEORGE
I'll be right down.

                    UNCLE BILLY
Go on, you'll miss the train -- You're
a week late for school already.

                     GEORGE
          (sharply)
Potter's motion.

                    UNCLE BILLY
Oh, don't worry -- so they put us out of
business. I'll get another job. I'm only
fifty-five --

                      TILLY
Fifty-six.

                    UNCLE BILLY
--go on--You gave up your boat trip, now
do you want to miss out on college too?
Go on!

                                        (CONTINUED)

                         DR. CAMPBELL'S VOICE
          George! George!

Dr. Campbell comes running out, all excited.

                         DR. CAMPBELL
          George, they voted Potter down.
          They want to keep it going!

                         UNCLE BILLY
          Whoopee!

                         GEORGE
          That's fine, Dr. Campbell. Goodbye.

                         DR. CAMPBELL
          You did it, George, you did it. But they
          got one condition -- only one condition --

                         UNCLE BILLY
               (disturbed)
          What's that?

                         DR. CAMPBELL
          That's the best part of it.
          They've appointed George here to be
          Executive Secretary -- to take his father's
          place!

                         GEORGE
          Oh, no! I can't -- Uncle Billy here!

                         DR. CAMPBELL
          You can keep him on -- that's all right --
          as Secretary, you can hire anyone you like.

                         GEORGE
          Wait a minute, Dr. Campbell -- Let's get
          this straight. I'm leaving -- for school --
          leaving right now. It's my last chance --
          here, Uncle Billy's your man.

                         DR. CAMPBELL
               (seriously)
          George, they'll vote with Potter otherwise.

                         GEORGE
          Doggone it, don't you people realize I've
          got plans -- I want to get away! Goodbye!

George runs out with his bags.

                                                    (CONTINUED)

> ERNIE
> (at door)
> We've only got a few minutes to make the
> train.

> DISSOLVE

Clarence and Joseph.

> CLARENCE
> You don't have to show me the rest. I
> know, I know -- he didn't go!

> JOSEPH
> That's right. Not only that, he gave his
> school money to his brother Harry and sent
> him to college. Harry became a football
> star. Made second team All-American.

> CLARENCE
> What happened to George?

> JOSEPH
> George? George got four years older,
> waiting for Harry to get back.

They look back at screen.

> DISSOLVE

EXT. RAILROAD STATION - DAY

MED. SHOT. Characteristic activity; a number of
townspeople waiting for the train. CAMERA MOVES UP
TO Uncle Billy and George. Uncle Billy munches
peanuts as George paces nervously up and down, glancing
up the tracks.

> UNCLE BILLY
> Relax, perpetual motion. It's
> only your brother we're meeting,
> you know.

> GEORGE
> (in high spirits)
> Not just my brother -- he's my
> deliverer! He's the Marines!
> He's that substitute that's going to
> carry the ball -- I've got it all fixed
> with the Board -- He's going to take my
> job! And I'm going to --
> (whistles)

> (CONTINUED)

                              UNCLE BILLY
                         (glumly)
                    Haven't you heard of the depression?
                    Where do you expect to get another job
                    in times like these?

                              GEORGE
                    Plenty of jobs for a man who
                    likes to travel!
                         (pulls some folders out
                          of his pockets)
                    Lookit here! Venezuela oil fields --
                    Wanted! -- Men with construction
                    experience.
                         (hearing approaching
                          train whistle)
                    Thar she blows! Know what the three
                    most exciting sounds in the world are?

                              UNCLE BILLY
                    Breakfast is served; lunch is served,
                    dinner --

                              GEORGE
                    No! Anchor chains -- plane motors --
                    and train whistles.

                              UNCLE BILLY
                         (sarcastic)
                    Peanut?

They move toward train.

                              UNCLE BILLY (cont'd)
                    Well, you won't be bothered with factory
                    whistles here for a while, anyway. Did
                    you hear they moved the last carload of
                    machinery out of the Tool and Dye Works
                    this afternoon?

George hasn't heard a word as he moves up platform.
Uncle Billy tags at his heels, chattering along.

                              UNCLE BILLY (cont'd)
                    Stripped the floors, lock, stock
                    and barrel. If this town hasn't hit
                    bottom yet, it's because there ain't
                    any bottom to this depression.

                                        (CONTINUED)

He stops as the train comes into shot. One or two
of the cars pass, then we catch a glimpse of Harry
on the platform of car. He sees George and Uncle
Billy, and waves excitedly. They wave back and
George turns and starts running in the same direction
as the train.

MED. SHOT. The train comes to a stop, and Harry is
among the first to get off, followed by an attractive
girl about the same age as he is. George rushes
into the shot, and as the brothers embrace:

                    GEORGE
              (joyously)
          Harry! Old Doctor, All-American,
          Professor Harry Phi Beta Kappa Bailey!

                    HARRY
          Well, if it isn't Old George
          Geographic Explorer Bailey!
              (looks around in mock
               surprise)
          What? No sled? No husky dogs?

Uncle Billy comes panting into shot.

                    HARRY (cont'd)
          Uncle Billy!
              (shakes hands)
          You haven't changed a bit.

                    UNCLE BILLY
          Nothing ever changes here, don't you
          know that?

                    HARRY
              (to George)
          Where's Mother?

                    GEORGE
          Home, cooking the fatted calf.
              (grabs Harry's arm,
               starts to yank him away)

                    HARRY
          Hey! Wait!

He stops and turns toward:

CLOSE SHOT - Ruth Dakin. This is the young lady who
came off the train with Harry. In the excitement of
greetings, she's been momentarily forgotten. She
stands smiling, waiting.

                                              (CONTINUED)

HARRY'S VOICE
George -- Uncle Bill -- I want you
to meet Ruth.

CLOSE SHOT - the group. Harry reaches for Ruth's
hand and brings her forward.

HARRY
Ruth Dakin.

RUTH
(demurely)
Ruth Dakin Bailey, if you don't mind.

George and Uncle Billy stare, astounded.

HARRY
(to George)
I wired you I had a surprise for you.
Well, here she is. Meet my wife.

George is thunderstruck. He takes Ruth's hand.

GEORGE
Well, how do you do.
Congratulations! Well, well,
well--

UNCLE BILLY
Well, what do you know -- what do
you know! Doggone, Harry, you can
certainly pick 'em. come on, let's
get going, Mrs. Bailey. I can't wait
to see everybody's eyes pop.

They start down platform. Harry and Ruth very much
pleased by the reception.

GEORGE
(to Ruth)
What ever made a pretty girl like you
marry this two-headed brother of mine?

RUTH
(smiling)
Purely mercenary. My father offered him
a job.

Uncle Billy smiles broadly as he realizes the
implication. George gets a sinking feeling. Harry
is slightly embarrassed.

(CONTINUED)

                              UNCLE BILLY
                        (to Ruth)
                  He gets you <u>and</u> a job? Harry's
                  cup runneth over.

Uncle Billy takes Ruth's arm and goes ahead. Harry
slows George down.

CLOSE SHOT - Harry and George walking.

                              HARRY
                  George -
                        (George doesn't answer)
                  - about that job - Ruth spoke out of
                  turn. I never said I'd take it. You've
                  been holding the bag for four years, and
                  I wouldn't let you down.
                        (George still doesn't ANSWER.
                         Harry suddenly remembers
                         something)
                  George, I do want to talk to you -
                  Gee, I forgot the bags.

Harry goes back to pick up the luggage. George crosses
to peanut stand where Uncle Billy is introducing Ruth
to the neighbors.

                              GEORGE
                  Harry'll be right back - he
                  forgot the bags.

                              RUTH
                  Good. George - George - George -
                  that's all he ever says. He did
                  so want to talk to you about the job.

                              GEORGE
                  What kind of a job is it?

                              RUTH
                  Dad owns a glassworks up in Buffalo.
                  He wants him to start in the research
                  department.

                              GEORGE
                  Good job?

                              RUTH
                  Wonderful - small money but big future
                  stuff. Dad fell in love with him.

                                          (CONTINUED)

                          GEORGE
And so did you?

                          RUTH (Laughs)
Dad's giving us a house to live in.
Naturally I hope Harry takes the job, but
he's being stubborn about it - says he's
got to talk to you first.

                          GEORGE
You tell him to take it and be darn
grateful and that I said he's lucky.

                          RUTH (Giggles)
Thanks.

She exits leaving George standing alone, as he hears
train whistle blow. Uncle Billy and the rest call for
George to hurry and get into car.

                                    DISSOLVE

EXT. FRONT PORCH - BAILEY HOUSE - THAT NIGHT

The overhead porch light is burning. It is summer.
The house is brilliantly lighted. Through the windows
can be seen about a dozen local young people. Harry
and Ruth are dancing to the radio. Outside, George
is sitting and smoking. His mother is knitting. Annie
is handing George a cocktail from tray. Uncle Billy
comes out of door, tipsy, hat on head. He feels very
high.

                          UNCLE BILLY
What a party! What a party! Hi there,
George, old boy, old boy, old boy.
Happy days, huh? Let them young fellers
go out and conquer the world. We old
timers stick together, eh, Georgie, old
boy, old boy. You certainly had me worried,
old pal.
     (to Ma Bailey)
Do you know what would have happened if
George left the Building and Loan?

                          MA BAILEY
     (trying to stop him)
Yes, we know.

                          UNCLE BILLY
You know, huh? Well, I'll tell you. First
they'd kick me right out on my ear -- they
think I'm an idiot, you know. Then Potter'd
move in,

                                    (CONTINUED)

                              UNCLE BILLY (cont'd)
                    (to Ma Bailey)
          And you'd be taking in boarders, Yes, sir.
          The Building and Loan would go -- just
          like that! And what would the world be
          like without our Building and Loan, huh?
          Oh boy, the place your poor father used
          to try to run like the Good Lord would
          run it -- I feel so good, I could spit in
          Potter's eye. Think I will, think I will,
          think I will.
                    (no one speaks)
          What'd you say?

Annie comes out onto porch.

                              UNCLE BILLY (cont'd)
          Yeah, well maybe I better go home.
          Where's my hat? Where's my hat?

George reaches up, takes his hat off his head and hands
it to him.

                              UNCLE BILLY (cont'd)
          Thanks, Annie. Which one is mine?

                              ANNIE
          The middle one.

                              UNCLE BILLY
          Good.
                    (puts hat on head)
          Now George, old pal, just point me in the
          right direction, will you, old pal?
                    (George gets up and goes with
                     him down steps)
          That way, huh? Thanks, thanks, old pal,
          old Building and Loan pal.

Billy starts to sing "My Wild Irish Rose."

                              UNCLE BILLY (cont'd)
          Say George, do you really make that bathtub
          gin in a bathtub?

                              GEORGE
          Sure thing. Every night but Saturday night.

                              UNCLE BILLY
          Every night, but Sat....

                              (CONTINUED)

He explodes in a violent fit of laughter as he
teeters away from house. Down sidewalk, there is
a loud crash o.s. as Uncle Billy falls over garbage
pail. George smiles and goes back upstairs to
Mrs. Bailey.

CLOSE SHOT. Ma Bailey and George. George sits
down again. Mrs. Bailey leans over and kisses him.
"That's for nothing."

                    MRS. BAILEY
          How do you like her?

                    GEORGE
          Oh, she's fine.

                    MRS. BAILEY
          Looks like she'll keep Harry on his toes.

                    GEORGE
          Keep him out of Bedford Falls, anyway.

                    MRS. BAILEY
               (pause)
          Did you know that Mary Hatch was back
          from school?

                    GEORGE
          Hm-m-m-m!

                    MA BAILEY
          Got back three days ago.

                    GEORGE
          HM-M-M-M!

                    MA BAILEY
          A nice girl, Mary.

                    GEORGE
          Mn-n-n.

                    MA BAILEY
          The kind that'll help you find the answers,
          George.

                    GEORGE
          M-n.

                    MOTHER
          Stop grunting.

                              (CONTINUED)

                              GEORGE
          M.

                              MOTHER
          Can you give me one good reason why
          you shouldn't call on Mary?

                              GEORGE
          Yep. Sam Wainwright.

                              MOTHER
               (derisively)
          Hee-haw.

                              GEORGE
          Sam's crazy about Mary.

                              MOTHER
          She isn't crazy about him.

                              GEORGE
          How do you know? Has she discussed
          it with you?

                              MOTHER
          No.

                              GEORGE
          Then how do you know?

                              MOTHER
          I've got eyes, haven't I? She lights
          up like a firefly when you're around.

                              GEORGE
          Blah!

                              MOTHER
          And besides, Sam Wainwright's away in New
          York, and you're here in Bedford Falls.

                              GEORGE
          And all's fair in love and war, huh?

                              MOTHER
               (primly)
          I don't know about war.

     George laughs, gets to his feet.

                                        (CONTINUED)

                         GEORGE
              Mother o'mine, I see right through
              you to your back collar button --
              want to get rid of me, don't you?

                         MOTHER
                   (fondly gives him his hat)
              Yes. George, here's your hat --
              what's your hurry?!

                         GEORGE
              I'll beat you over the head with a
              baseball bat.
                   (kisses her -- looks up and sees
                   Harry and wife inside)

He goes to the edge of the porch, looks up at the
star-studded sky. Annie listens in from the doorway.

                         GEORGE (cont'd)
              A lot of stars out tonight...Did you
              know that the nearest star is over
              twenty-five trillion miles away from the
              earth?

CLOSEUP - Mother. Her face suddenly sad and wistful
as she looks toward George.

                         GEORGE'S VOICE
              Gosh, that'd be some trip, wouldn't it?

MED. SHOT.

                         ANNIE
                   (moves into scene)
              If you're going that far, better take
              your hat.
                   (holds out his hat)

                         GEORGE
              Sure, Annie, old pal, old pal.
                   (imitating Uncle Billy)
              Which one's mine?

                         ANNIE
              The end one.

George grabs an imaginary end hat, put his on his head.

                              (CONTINUED)

                    GEORGE
        Think I'll go out and do some
        passionate necking, Ma, just point
        me in the right direction, will you,
        old pal?

Mother turns him in what is evidently Mary's direction.

                    GEORGE (cont'd)
            (smiling)
        Oh, no.
            (Starts singing "Wild
            Irish Rose.")

He turns in opposite direction and walks off. Mother
looks after him wistfully.

                    ANNIE
        You know, Mrs. Bailey, I wouldn't
        be surprised if that Mary Hatch didn't
        turn out to be an old maid. She's kind
        of iceberg-like.

                    MRS. BAILEY
        Well, most women are icebergs until they
        hit their Gulf stream.

                    ANNIE
        I sure hope I hurry and find my Gulf
        stream.

EXT. STREET - NIGHT

CLOSE MOVING SHOT - George. Hatless, he walks along,
his feet on the ground, but his eyes on the remote
stars. Under his breath, he's muttering:

                    GEORGE
        Yep, yep, yep, yep.

He pauses suddenly to look at:

EXT. BUILDING AND LOAN ASSOCIATION OFFICE - NIGHT

CLOSE SHOT at entrance. A sign. It reads:

    BEDFORD FALLS BUILDING & LOAN ASSOCIATION

George comes into shot and look at the sign as if for
the first time.

                                    (CONTINUED)

EXT. STREET - NIGHT

CLOSE MOVING SHOT. Ernie is cruising in his taxi.
O.s. he sees George, stops the cab at the curb, gets
out and starts over.

CLOSE SHOT - George and Ernie.

                    ERNIE
          Hello, George.

                    GEORGE
              (turning)
          Hello, Ernie.
              (stares at the sign again)
          What do you know about that?
          Ever noticed that before?

He points to the word "BUILDING" and we see that the
"L" is missing.

                    GEORGE (cont'd)
          Somebody's knocked the "L" out of
          "BUILDING."

                    ERNIE
          Sombody's knocked the "L" out of
          Taxi, too.
              (fumbles, then abruptly)
          I was coming in to see you in the morning -

                    GEORGE
          You know somebody wants to buy a
          nice Building and Loan Association --
          in not so good running condition?

They look at each other glumly.

                    GEORGE (cont'd)
          How about a swap?
              (shakes his head)
          No, I wouldn't do that to you.
          What's on your mind, Ernie?

                    ERNIE
          Well - what I wanted to say was - I was
          coming in in the morning to give you the
          deed to my house. I can't make the payments
          on it any more. 'Bout the only time you
          get a fare nowadays is when some guy takes
          his wife to the hospital for more kids. I
          can't charge a guy for that. It'll be a
          little tough on the missus, but we figured
          we'd move in with her folks.

                        GEORGE
Ernie, do you think you could manage
to pay the interest on the loan --
just the interest?

                        ERNIE
Sure I can do that, but --

                        GEORGE
You keep the house, Ernie. Forget the
principal for the time being. Pay the
interest. We know you -- and keep the
deed.

                        ERNIE
            (blubbering)
Gee, George - gee --
            (puts deed back
             into pocket)
Excuse me - think I'll run on home.
The missus'll be very happy.
            (he runs toward his cab)

                    OFF SCENE VOICE
Taxi!

                        ERNIE
            (yelling)
Be right up.
            (to George)
I'm back in business.
            (he exits)

MED. SHOT - front of Violet Bick's Beauty Shop. It
looks like a new shop. A sign on it reads:

        VI'S BEAUTY SHOPPE

Violet is locking up for the night. A couple of men -
apparently her last two customers -- are crowding around
her, each one bent on taking her out. There is laughter,
kidding and pawing.

                        MEN
            (ad lib)
Vi, you promised me tonight --
I called you this morning, Honey --
I got a table waiting, Vi --
Now, look, who got it for you wholesale, huh?

                                        (CONTINUED)

                              VIOLET
                          (ad lib)
                   Now wait a minute -- take it easy
                   -- one at a time -- and no hands,
                   please --

O.s. she sees George walking alone.

                              VIOLET (cont'd)
                   Oh-oh. Excuse me, boys -- I think
                   I've got a date -- but hang around
                   fellows, just in case --

She exits in George's direction.

CLOSE SHOT - George and Violet. Violet comes up and
takes George's arm.

                              VIOLET
                   Why, Georgie-Porgie!

                              GEORGE
                   Hi, Vi.

He looks her over. Violet takes her beauty shop
seriously and she's an eyeful. She senses the fact
that George is far from immune to her attractions.
She links her arm in his and continues on down the
street with him.

CLOSE MOVING SHOT - George and Violet. Behind them,
the two men follow.

                              GEORGE
                   How's ye old-fashioned permanent
                   wave shoppe?

                              VIOLET
                   Well, it's not a tidal wave, yet, but
                   I'm getting some of the city mothers in
                   -- thanks to you. Got the fish-eye when
                   I tried to put an ad in the paper though.
                   The old geezer said I should call it a
                   barbershop. Georgie, can I help it if
                   they hang around?

                              GEORGE
                   You can't help it -- and they can't help
                   it either. After all, it's the vernal
                   equinox.

                                                    (CONTINUED)

                              VIOLET
          Huh?

                              GEORGE
          When the sap rises in the trees that's--

He becomes aware of the two men walking behind them.

                         GEORGE (cont'd)
          Who are the saps?

                              VIOLET
               (carelessly)
          Oh, a couple of vernal equinoxes.
          Where are you going?

                              GEORGE
          Oh, going to the library, I guess.

                              VIOLET
          Georgie, don't you ever get tired of
          reading about things?

Her eyes are seductive and guileful as she looks up
at him. He is silent for a moment, then blurts out:

                              GEORGE
          Yeah - what are you doing tonight?

                              VIOLET
               (feigned surprise)
          Why, not a thing.

                              GEORGE
          Are you game, Vi? Let's make a night of
          it -- I've got to talk to somebody. Let's
          go out in the fields. We'll take off our
          shoes and walk through the grass. Then
          we'll go to the falls - they're beautiful
          in the moonlight -- there's a pool there -
          a green pool -
               (looking around to see
                that nobody is listening)
          - and we can swim in it. Then we'll climb
          Mt. Bedford - and smell the pines - and
          watch the sunrise hit the peaks. What do
          you say, Vi? We'll stay out the whole
          night, and everybody'll talk - and there'll
          be a terific scandal -- What do you say?

                              VIOLET
          George, have you lost your mind? Walk
          through the grass in my bare feet?

                                        (CONTINUED)

There is offscene laughter from bystanders who have
stopped to listen to their quarrel.

>   VIOLET (cont'd)
>   Why it's ten miles to Befored Falls and
>   this is the only thing I've got to
>   wear. You want me to go swimming in this?

Offscene laguther.

>   GEORGE
>   Oh let's forget about the whole thing.

He starts to exit.

>   VIOLET
>   (as he goes)
>   You're a funny guy - what's the matter
>   with you?

The people start to laugh and move away as the two
mashers enter scene.

>   VIOLET (cont'd)
>   (still in a daze)
>   You know what he wanted me to do?
>   (with rising force)
>   Do you like to walk thorugh the grass in
>   your bare feet? No! Do you ask me to
>   swim in the moonlight? No! Do you want
>   me to smell the pines and watch the sunrise
>   hit the peaks? No! All you want me to
>   do is dance and to drink and to neck!
>   (kicking violently at
>   one of the masher's shins)
>   Well, get out! Beat it! Let me alone!
>   This is one night I'm going home.

She starts up the street in a determined walk, leaving
the wolf nursing his shin.

>   DISSOLVE

EXT. SIDE STREET - NIGHT

MED. SHOT - George comes into shot, approaches one
of the houses, and stops to look at it, stick in hand.

>   (CONTINUED)

CLOSER ANGLE - George stares mediatively at the simple
dwelling, then he starts walking ahead. But after
a few steps he turns around and starts back. He
walks past the house a few yards, turns and starts
back again.

CLOSE (MOVING) SHOT - George, his head sunk deep
in thought, as he approaches the house. As he passes:

                    MARY'S VOICE
          What are you doing -- picketing?

George stops, startled, and looks up toward:

CLOSE SHOT - at window. It is open, and back of
the curtain gently billowing in the mild breeze, we
catch glimpse of Mary.

                    GEORGE'S VOICE
          Oh, hello Mary.

He comes into shot.

                    GEORGE
          I just happened to be passing by...

                    MARY
          Yes, so I noticed. Have you made up
          your mind?

                    GEROGE
          How's that?

                    MARY
          Have you made up your mind?

                    GEORGE
               (frightened)
          About what?

                    MARY
               (innocently)
          About coming in. Your mother just
          telephoned and said you were on your way
          over to pay me a visit.

                    GEORGE
          Mother called you? How did she know?

                    MARY
          Didn't you tell her?

                         GEORGE
          No, I didn't tell anybody. I just
          started out from the house for a walk
          and happened to be passing by.

But she has disappeared from the window.

INT.   HATCH HOME

Mary comes running downstairs. Quickly turns on
Victrola with George's favorite record. She is
plainly excited at George's visit as she goes to the
door.

EXT.   DOOR

George is hanging back, sore at being told he was
expected.

                         MARY
          Well, are you coming in or aren't you?

                         GEORGE
          Well just a minute -- but I didn't
          tell anybody I was coming over here, you
          know.

He enters the house.

INT. LIVING ROOM - HATCH HOME

FULL SHOT - a simple, comfortable home, the same type
and period as the Bailey home. George and Mary enter
from the hallway.

                         GEORGE
                    (as they enter)
          When did you get back?

                         MARY
          Tuesday.

                         GEORGE
          Where'd you get that dress?

                         MARY
          Do you like it?

                         GEORGE
          It's all right. I thought you'd go on
          to New York like Sam, and Ingie, and the
          rest.

                                              (CONTINUED)

                         MARY
          I worked there a couple of vacations.
          But I don't know -- I guess I was
          homesick.

                         GEORGE
               (shocked)
          Homesick?   For Bedford Falls?

                         MARY
          Yes -- and my family -- and --
          Oh, everything. Would you like to sit
          down?

                         GEORGE
          Well, for just a minute -- I see the
          place still smells like pine needles.

                         MARY
          Would you like some tea and cake?

                         GEORGE
          No thanks.

A long pause.

                         MARY
          Get my letters?

                         GEORGE
          Yep, yep. Get mine?

                         MARY
          Ye, yep. Both of them.

                         GEORGE
          How's your brother, Marty?

                         MARY
          Oh, he joined a big law firm in Washington.
          Gets married next month.

                         GEORGE
          That's fine.

                         MARY
               (starts to sing)
          And dance by the light.

                         GEORGE
          What's the matter?
               (gets it)
          Oh.

                         MARY
          Nice about your brother Harry and
          Ruth, isn't it?

                         GEORGE
          Huh? Yeah - fine.

                         MARY
          Don't you like her?

                         GEORGE
          Sure I do - she's a peach.

                         MARY
          Just marriage in general you're not
          enthusiastic about, huh?

                         GEORGE
          Oh, no - it's all right for Harry and
          Marty, and Sam --
               (pauses)
          -- and Sam and you --

                    MRS. HATCH'S VOICE
               (from stairway)
          Mary! Who's down there with you?

                         MARY
          It's George Bailey, mother.

                    MRS. HATCH'S VOICE
          George Bailey? What's he want?

                         MARY
          I don't know.
               (to George
                mischievously)
          What do you want?

                         GEORGE
               (rising)
          Me? Nothing, nothing! I - I just
          came in to get warm.

                         MARY
               (to mother)
          He's making violent love to me, mother.

George is aghast.

                                        (CONTINUED)

                              MRS. HATCH'S VOICE
          You tell him to go right back home, and
          don't you leave the house either. Sam
          Wainwright promised to call you from
          New York tonight.

                              MARY
          Yes, mother. What were you saying,
          George?

                              GEORGE
               (heatedly)
          Lookit here - your mother needn't --
          I didn't come here to - to - to -

                              MARY
               (rising)
          What did you come here for then?

                              GEORGE
               (heatedly)
          I don't know! You tell me -
          you're supposed to be the one that knows
          all the answers - you tell me.

                              MARY
               (terribly hurt)
          Oh, why don't you go home?

Telephone starts ringing.

                              GEORGE
          I will. Shouldn't have come here in
          the first place. Good night!

                              MARY
          Good night!

                              MRS. HATCH
          Good night!

                              GEORGE
          Good night!

                              MRS. HATCH
               (in dressing gown at
                top of stairs)
          Mary! Mary!

                              MARY
          What is it, mother?

                                      (CONTINUED)

                              MRS. HATCH
            The telephone!   It's Sam!

                              MARY
            I'll get it.

                              MRS. HATCH
            Whatever were you doing that you
            couldn't hear?

Mary breaks record.   She goes to phone in hall.   George
comes back in.

                              GEORGE
            I forgot my hat!

                              MARY
                 (overly enthusiastic)
            Hello.

                              SAM'S VOICE
                 (over phone)
            Hee-haw -- hee haw!   It's good to hear
            your voice again.

                              MARY
            Oh, hello Sam - how are you?
                 (glances toward door, sees
                  George still there)
            That's awfully sweet of you, Sam.   There's
            a friend of yours here....George Bailey....
            yes, old moss-back, George.

                              SAM'S VOICE
            Hee-haw!   Put him on.

                              MARY
            Wait a minute.   I'll get him.

She puts down the receiver.   Her mother looks daggers
at her.

                              MRS. HATCH
                 (in a fierce whisper)
            He doesn't want to speak to George.

                              MARY
            He does so!   He asked for him.
                 (calls out)
            Oh, George!   Sam wants to talk to you!

                                        (CONTINUED)

Her mother rolls her eyes to heaven, then scuttles back up the stairs again. George enters from the living room.

                    MARY (cont'd)
              (into phone)
          Here he is.

She hands over the instrument to George.

INT. SAM'S OFFICE IN NEW YORK

CLOSE SHOT - Sam on phone. On the desk before him are papers spread out, with blueprints and so forth.

                    SAM
          Well, George Bailoffski! What're you trying
          to do? Steal my girl? What is this?

INT.   HATCH HALLWAY

CLOSE SHOT - George and Mary. George looks uncomfortably at Mary.

                    GEORGE
          What're you talking about - nobody's
          trying to steal your girl.

He starts to give the telephone back to Mary, but Sam's voice stops him.

                    SAM'S VOICE
              (over phone)
          Wait a minute. I want to talk to both
          of you. Tell Mary to get on the
          extension.

                    MARY
          Mother's on the other extension.

                    MOTHER
          I am not!

                    MARY
          Come on - we can both hear!

Mary takes the telephone from George and holds it so that of necessity George's cheek is almost against hers. He is very conscious of her proximity.

(CONTINUED)

                         MARY (cont'd)
               (on phone)
          We're listening, Sam.

INT. SAM'S OFFICE

CLOSE SHOT - Sam.

                         SAM
               (on phone)
          I've got a big deal coming up that's
          going to make us all rich. Remember
          that night in Martini's bar when you
          told me about making plastics out of
          soybeans?
               (then as they
                don't answer)
          You remember - soy beans?

BACK TO GEORGE AND MARY. George shakes himself out
of his preoccupation with Mary.

                         GEORGE
          Huh? Yeah - yeah - soybeans.

                         SAM
          Well, Dad snapped up the idea. He's
          going to build a factory outside Rochester
          -- How do you like that?

                         GEORGE
          Rochester? Why Rochester?

                         SAM
          Have you got any better ideas?

INT. HATCH HALLWAY

CLOSE SHOT - George and Mary. Mary is watching George
interestedly. George is very conscious of her, close
to him.

                         GEORGE
          Why not right here? Remember the Tool
          Machinery Works? Tell your father he
          can get that for a song. And all the
          labor he needs. Half the town was
          thrown out of work when they closed down.

                         SAM'S VOICE
          That so? I'll talk to him. Sounds good!
          I knew you'd come through, baby! Now
          here's the point - and I want Mary to get
          in on this, too - Got any money?

                                        (CONTINUED)

                              GEORGE
          Money? Yeah, a little.

                          SAM'S VOICE
          Yeah - put every dime you've got into
          our stock, you hear?

                              GEORGE
          Thanks a lot, Sam - I --

                          SAM'S VOICE
          Might even have a job for you, George --
          unless you're still married to that
          broken down old bldg. & loan. This is
          the biggest thing since radio. And we're
          letting you in on the ground floor.
          Mary...Mary...Are you listening, honey?

                              MARY
               (coming closer)
          I'm here.

                          SAM'S VOICE
          Tell him I'm giving him the chance of
          a lifetime, you hear? The chance of
          a lifetime!
               (there is no answer
                from line)
          That's funny. Must've hung up. I'll
          call back later.

He starts out of office with friends.

INT. MARY'S HOUSE

As Mary listens, she turns to look at George, her lips
almost on his lips.

                              MARY
               (whispering)
          He says it's the chance of a lifetime.

George looks at her.

Suddenly he grabs her by the shoulders, fiercely,
dropping phone.

                              GEORGE
          I don't want any plastics. I don't want
          any ground floors. And I don't want to
          get married -- ever -- to anyone! I want
          to do what I want to do, you hear? And
          you're not going to -- you're -- you're
          ...I...I...Oh, Mary...Mary.

                                              (CONTINUED)

He pulls her to him in a fierce embrace. Two meant
for each other find themselves in tearful ecstasy.

CLOSE SHOT - Mrs. Hatch at top of stairs. She
practically faints at the sight.

                                        DISSOLVE

INT. HALLWAY - BIALEY HOUSE (OCTOBER AFTERNOON, 1932)

MED. SHOT. From the living room comes the SOUND of
an organ and harp, playing the Wedding March. The
people are crowded into the rooms; family, friends,
neighbors. There is a din of conversation. Mary and
George appear at the top of the stairs in traveling
clothes, with Mrs. Hatch, red-eyed, behind them. A
scream goes up from Ruth in the living room.

                    RUTH
        Here they are! Quick, they're going.

The people start to surge from the living room. We
notice that Uncle Billy is not among them. Mary
makes a dash for the front door. George comes down
after her, gives his mother a kiss and dodges out,
followed by people throwing rice. A misty drizzle
is falling. Those outside have umbrellas.

CLOSE SHOT - Mrs. Bailey and Annie. They stand
looking after George and Mary.

                    MRS. BAILEY
        First Harry. Now George. Annie, we're
        two old maids now.

                    ANNIE
        Speak for youself, Mrs. B.

EXT. HOUSE

FULL SHOT. Ernie's cab is standing at the curb.
It is covered with white ribbons, old shoes and
tin cans. On the back is written in soap, "JUST
MARRIED." Mary and George run down, pelted by
rice, and get in and drive quickly away. They turn
the corner of the street.

INT. CAB - AFTERNOON - LIGHT MIST FALLING

George, Mary and Ernie. George and Mary are in each
other's arms.

                                        (CONTINUED)

                              ERNIE
                    If you happen to see a stranger around
                    here, it's me.

George and Mary laugh.

                              GEORGE
                    Mary, somebody's driving this thing.

                              ERNIE
                         (handing them bottle
                          of champagne with ribbon)
                    From Bert the cop. Says to tell you to
                    float away to happyland on the bubbles.

                              GEORGE
                    Champagne! Good old Bert.

                              ERNIE
                    Hate to be inquisitive, but what'll I
                    tell the wife when she asks me where you
                    two are going on this here now honeymoon?

                              GEORGE
                    Where we going?
                         (takes out a fat roll
                          of bills)
                    See this? The old kitty.
                    Count it, Mary.

                              MARY
                    Ha! I feel like a bootlegger's wife!

                              GEORGE
                    Know what we're going to do? Shoot the
                    works. A whole week in New York! A
                    whole week in Bermuda! The highest hotel
                    -- the oldest champagne -- the richest
                    caviar -- the hottest music -- and the
                    prettiest wife.

                              ERNIE
                    That does it! Then what?

                              GEORGE
                         (to Mary)
                    Then what, honey?

                              MARY
                    After that, who cares?

                                         (CONTINUED)

                              GEORGE
          That does it! Come here!
                    (embraces her; then
                     looking around at the
                     town with an exaggerated
                     villain's leer)
          Goodbye, Bedford Falls -- goodbye,
          Building and Loan -- Potter --
          Uncle Billy and all the rest of you --
          we're sneaking out and we're never
          coming back --

Ernie starts singing, "As I was Walking Down the
Street." George and Mary join in. Ernie weaves
the cab from side to side in tempo with the song.
They pass the bank. Still singing, Ernie leans to
look back. He sees a crowd around the bank door.
His song fades as he stops cab. George and Mary
continue singing.

                              ERNIE
          Don't look now -- but something's going
          on at the bank.

George and Mary stop and look back.

                         ERNIE (cont'd)
          I've never seen one, but that has all
          the earmarks of a run.

LONG SHOT - scurrying people under umbrellas,
swarming around bank doors. Panic is in the air.
Attendants are trying to close down. Several people
come running by cab.

                            PASSERBY
          Ernie, got any money in the bank?
          Better hurry!

                             MARY
          George, let's not stop -- let's go!
          Let's go!

                            GEORGE
          Just a minute, dear.

He looks down the street at entrance to Building and
Loan. He sees smaller crowd around entrance.

                            GEORGE
          Oh, oh.

                                          (CONTINUED)

George gets out of cab.

                        MARY
          George, please let's not <u>stop</u>.

                        GEORGE
          Back in a second, dear.

George runs toward Building and Loan.

EXT. BUILDING AND LOAN

An iron grill blocks the street entrance to the
Building and Loan. It has been locked. About
fifteen men and women are waiting around rattling
the grill. They are simply dressed people, to whom
their savings are a matter of life and death.

George comes in, with an assumed cheerful manner.
The people look at him silently, half shamefaced,
but grimly determined on their rights. In their
hearts there is panic and fear.

                        GEORGE
          Hello everybody. Mrs. Thompson, how
          are you? Charlie? What's the matter,
          can't you get in?

No one answers. He quickly unlocks the grill door
and pushes it open.
                        GEORGE
          There you are.
                (enters first)
          Come on in.
The crowd pushes through.

INT. BUILDING AND LOAN

George goes up the stairs two at a time. The crowd
follows him like a herd, right behind him.

INT. SECOND FLOOR - OUTSIDE DOOR TO OFFICE

George finds entrance door locked. He takes out keys.
Crowd surrounds him.

                        GEORGE
                (an attempt at humor)
          You'd think we had a lot of money
          in here - with all these locks.

                        (CONTINUED)

No one laughs. George opens door and enters. The
help is standing back of counter, stony-faced.
Uncle Billy, 'way back in his office, is surprised
in the act of taking a nap. He hurriedly puts bottle
away and comes out into main office.

                    GEORGE
          Hello, Uncle Billy, what's this - a
          holiday?
                (to mob)
          Come on in, come on in.
                (as he starts for inner
                  office)
          Why don't you all sit down and be
          comfortable? Plenty of seats.

                    UNCLE BILLY
          George, can I see you a minute?

He points to George's office. George turns back
cheerfully to crowd. The people ignore this but
remain standing in front of teller's window. They
all have their pass books out.

George hurries into his office. Uncle Billy is
anxiously waiting for him.

                    GEORGE
          Why didn't you call me?

                    UNCLE BILLY
          I just did. They said you'd left. Nice
          pickle, George, nice pickle.

                    GEORGE
          How did it start? What happened?

                    UNCLE BILLY
          How does anything like this start? All
          I know is the bank called our loan --

                    GEORGE
          When?

                    UNCLE BILLY
          An hour ago. I had to hand over all
          our cash.

                    GEORGE
          All of it? You know what those people
          want out there? They want their money.

                                        (CONTINUED)

                         UNCLE BILLY
          Then I got scared and closed the doors --

George brushes it out mechanically, his mind on his
problem.

                         GEROGE
                    (looking out window)
          The whole town's gone crazy.

The telephone rings. Billy picks it up.

                         BILLY
                    (on phone)
          Hello? George, it's Potter.

CLOSE SHOT - Potter, in his office. Seated at the
side of the desk is a distinguished-looking man,
evidently the president of the bank. He sits
miserably wiping the sweat from his forehead.

                         POTTER
                    (showing great concern)
          George, are you all right? Need any
          police?

                         GEORGE
          Police? What for?

                         POTTER
                    (all out to sound sincere)
          George, I'm going all out to help in
          this crisis. I've just guaranteed sufficient
          funds to meet the needs at the bank. They'll
          close down for a week -- and then reopen.

                         GEORGE
                    (to Uncle Billy)
          He's just taken over the bank.
                    (back to Potter)
          Under new management, I suppose.

                         POTTER
                    (with a glance at the distracted
                     bank manager beside him)
          Well - slightly.
                    (to bank manger)
          Mr. Parker, you may return to our bank.

Bank manger leaves.

                                              (CONTINUED)

                              POTTER
                     (continues on
                      telephone)
              Now George, I may lose a fortune but
              I'm willing to guarantee your people too.
              Have them bring their shares to me and
              I'll pay fifty cents on the dollar.

                              GEORGE
              Not a chance, Mr. Potter, we don't
              believe in fire sales over here.

                              POTTER
              What are you going to do?

                              GEORGE
              Do? I'm going to tell them the truth,
              that's what I'm going to do.

                              POTTER
              The truth is you haven't any cash and you
              know it. You'll go into bankruptcy and
              your people will lose everything. Is that
              what you want? You're always trying to
              help the working man, now I'm trying to
              help you. If your doors close before six
              P.M., you'll never reopen.

                              GEORGE
              You don't miss a trick, do you, Potter?
              Well you're going to miss this one.
                     (he hangs up - turns to
                      Uncle Billy)
              Now what are we going to do?

                              UNCLE BILLY
              George, you've got a little rice in your
              hair. Was it a nice wedding? Gosh, I
              wanted to be there.

                              GEORGE
                     (indicates string on Uncle
                      Billy's little finger)
              Yeah - you can take that one off now.

An ominous SOUND of angry voices comes from the other
room. SOUNDS of rattling window bars and clamors for
action. George and Uncle Billy exit to the main room.

INT. OUTER OFFICE - BUILDING AND LOAN

                                           (CONTINUED)

More people have crowded around the receiving window,
making about thirty. Their muttering stops and they
stand silent and grim. There is panic in their faces.
Mary has come in and meets George as he and Uncle
Billy come in from George's office. George pats her
and goes right to people. Mary watches the following
scene silently. A siren blows outside, which excites
people.

                    GEORGE
              (from behind
               counter)
         I suppose you're all here for the same
         reason. You want your money. This
         thing isn't as bad as it looks right now.
         I just talked to Potter on the phone and
         the bank's going to open next week.

                    ED
         I got my money here.

                    CHARLIE
         Did he guarantee this place?

                    GEORGE
         I didn't ask him to; we don't need him --

                    CHARLIE
         Then I'll take mine.

                    GEORGE
         You're thinking of this place all wrong.
         As if I were keeping your money in a
         safe back here. Your money isn't here.
         It's in Joe's house...
              (to one of the
               men)
         ...right next to yours. And in Kenny's
         house, and the Macklins...and a hundred
         others. You lent them the money to build
         and they're paying you back as best they
         can. What do you want to do? Foreclose
         on them? Throw them out?

                    NICK
         I got two hundred and forty-two dollars
         in here. Two hundred and forty-two
         isn't going to break anyone.

                    GEORGE
              (handing him slip)
         Okay -- sign this. You'll get it in
         sixty days.

                                        (CONTINUED)

                              NICK
              Sixty days!

                              GEORGE
              That's what you agred to when you bought
              your shares.

There is a commotion at the outer doors. A man (Randall)
comes in and makes his way up to Charlie.

                              RANDALL
                    (excitedly)
              Charlie...did you get your money?

                              NICK
              No.

                              RANDALL
              I just did. Potter'll pay you fifty
              cents on the dollar -- for your shares -
              look -- cash!
                    (shows bills)

                              NICK
                    (to George)
              Well, what do you say?

                              GEORGE
              You'll have to stick by your agreement
              ...give us sixty days.

                              NICK
                    (turning to Randall)
              Okay, Randall.

He starts out.

                              MRS. THOMPSON
                    (to Nick)
              You going to go to Potter?

                              NICK
              Better to get half than nothing.

A few other people start for the door. George comes
out from behind the counter quickly, speaking to the
people.

                              GEORGE
              Listen...Nick...Tom...Listen, everyone.
              I'm begging you not to do this. If Potter
              gets hold of this Building and Loan, there'll
              never be another decent house built in this
              town.

                                        (CONTINUED)

                          GEORGE (cont'd)
He's taken over the bank, the bus lines.
He's got the department store. And now
he's out to get us. Why? Because we're
cutting into his business. Because he'd
like to keep you living in his slums,
paying the rents that _he_ decides.

The people are still trying to get out -- but one or
two have stood still, listening to him. George has
begun to make an impression on them.

                          GEORGE (cont'd)
Nick...you lived in one of his houses.
Have you forgotten it? Have you
forgotten what you used to pay for that
broken down shack?
       (to Ed)
Ed! Remember last year when things were
tough, and you couldn't always pay?
You didn't lose your new house, did you?
Do you think that Potter would have let
you keep it?
        (turns to address
         the room again)
Can't you see? Potter isn't selling -
he's _buying_! Why? Because we're panicky
and he's not -- and he's picking up
bargains. We'll pull through somehow - all
we have to do is stick together - have
faith in each other.

                        MRS. THOMPSON
My husband's out of work a year now.
I need money.

                        ANOTHER WOMAN
What am I going to live on 'till the
bank opens?

                        FIRST MAN
I have a doctor's bill to pay.

                        SECOND MAN
I need cash -- gotta have cash!

                        THIRD MAN
Can't feed my kids on faith!

During this scene Mary has joined George. Suddenly
she slips the roll of bills in George's hand. George
glances at it -- gets the idea. He throws roll of
bills into a wire backet.

                                      (CONTINUED)

                              MARY
               How much do you need?

                             GEORGE
               Hey -- wait. I have two thousand dollars
               here. My own money. That ought to tide
               us over 'till the bank reopens.
                         (to Nick, the first
                          in line)
               Now, how much could you do with?

                              NICK
                         (doggedly)
               I'll take my two hundred and forty-two
               dollars.

George starts rapidly to count out the money. Charlie
throws his passbook on the counter.

                          NICK (cont'd)
               That'll clean out my account.

                             GEORGE
               Your account's still here. This is a
               loan.

Mary turns and slips out through the crowd. He hands
the two hundred and forty-two dollars to Nick and
speaks to Ed, the next in line. Nick grabs his book
and leaves, carefully counting his money.

                         GEORGE (cont'd)
                         (to Ed)
               What do you need, Ed?

                               ED
               I got three hundred here.

Uncle Billy gets out his wallet and takes out all the
cash he's got.

                             GEORGE
                         (doggedly)
               What do you need 'till the bank reopens?

                               ED
               I suppose, twenty --

                             GEORGE
                         (giving it to him)
               That's better.
                         (to Mrs. Thompson, next
                          in line)
               Now, Mrs. Thompson.

                                              (CONTINUED)

                         MRS. THOMPSON
          It's your own money.

                         GEORGE
          That doesn't matter.

Cousin Eustice and Tilly dash in.

                         EUSTICE
          Uncle Billy! Uncle Billy, there's a
          run on the bank!

                         UNCLE BILLY
          What do you think's going on here?

                         TILLY
               (runs to phone)
          Wait'll I tell Martha about this.

                         MRS. THOMPSON
          I can get along with twenty, too.
               (as George counts
                it out)
          I'll sign a paper.

                         GEORGE
               (giving her money)
          I know you'll pay me back when you can.
               (to woman next in
                line)
          Mrs. Davis?

                         MRS. DAVIS
          Could I have thirty-seven fifty?

                         GEORGE
          Just a minute.
               (as he starts
                to count)
          Take only what you need, folks -
          let's spread this thin.

                         NICK
          Oh, George, I don't need all this --
          I'll give you two hundred dollars back.

                                        DISSOLVE OUT

INT. BLDG. AND LOAN

The lights are on, but still a little daylight outside.
George, Uncle Billy, Eustice and Tilly -- all coatless
and disheveled. George at cashier window, looking at
wall clock and counting the seconds.

                                        (CONTINEUD)

                        GEORGE
           nine...eight...seven.

Uncle Billy and Tilly in back of him, in tense excitement.

                     UNCLE BILLY
           We're going to make it, George --
           they'll never close us up today.

Cousin Eustace at door waiting for the word to close it.
Sign on door reads "9 to 6."

                        GEORGE
              Three...two...one -- BINGO!

Cousin Eustace slams door and locks it. Cheers from
Uncle Billy and Tilly.

                     GEORGE (cont'd)
           We made it! -- We're still in business
                 (waving two one dollar bills
                  in the air)
           We've still got two bucks left. A
           couple of financial wizards, eh, Uncle
           Billy.

                     UNCLE BILLY
           Huh, those Rockefellers!

                        GEORGE
           Uncle Billy, break out what you've got
           in that hip pocket. Cousin Tilly, glasses.
           We've got to celebrate. Cousin Eustace,
           a tray for these two big important simoleons.

                     UNCLE BILLY
           We'll save them for seed - A toast!
           A toast!

                        GEORGE
           To Papa Dollar and Mama Dollar! If you
           want the old Building and Loan to stay in
           business hurry up and have a family.

                        TILLY
           I wish they were rabbits.

Making a noise like a band they march to the big, open
safe with the two dollars on the tray and go inside.
Eustace waits outside and passes out cigars as they
come out.

                                      (CONTINUED)

                         EUSTACE
          Wedding cigars!

                         GEORGE
          Wedding! Jeepers -- I'm married!
          Where's Mary?

                         TILLY
          George, call for you.

                         GEORGE
               (running to her)
          Get my wife -- at her mother's house!

                         TILLY
          Mrs. Bailey's on the line.

                         GEORGE
          I don't want Mrs. Bailey - I want my
          wife - oh, it is my wife!...Mary! Mary!
          Hello dear - listen, I'm sorry -- what?
          Come home - What home" Three twenty
          Sycamore? Whose home is that? The
          Waldorf Hotel?

                                        DISSOLVE

Before George arrives on scene, we find Bert, the
cop, urging on a paper-hanger to complete covering
broken windows with travel posters, etc., to keep
out the pouring rain. We see Ernie helping and
standing guard inside. Ad lib dialogue.

EXT. GRANVILLE HOUSE

An old-fashioned, run-down house, unpainted and
warped by the weather. It once had class but has not
been lived in for years. This is the house George
and Mary will live in from now on. The rain is
coming down. A faint glow of light shines out from
bottom windows. George hurries into scene. He stops
to make sure it is the right number before going up
steps. He goes up to the old-fashioned ornate door.
A large bronze knocker is on the door. Within the
knocker, a typewritten card is tacked on, reading:

     "BRIDAL SUITE."

George knocks with the knocker.

A small port-hole panel opens, revealing Ernie's face
topped by a high hat.

                                        (CONTINUED)

ERNIE
Ah, the groom! Entray, entray!

Ernie opens door, revealing himself as a home-made
butler. This he has accomplished by rolling up his
pants, and putting on an old coachman's hat. George
enters.

LIVING ROOM

George enters. The house is carpetless, empty -- the
rain and wind cause funny noises upstairs. A huge
fire is burning in the fireplace. Near the fireplace
a collection of packing boxes are heaped together in
the shape of a small table and covered with a checkered
oil cloth. It is set for two. A bucket with ice and
a champagne bottle sit on the table as well as a bowl
of caviar. Two small chickens are impaled on a spit
over the fire. A phonograph is playing on the box.
It is playing "The Wedding March." In front of phonograph is a sign reading, "Guy Lombardo." Mary is
standing near the fireplace looking as pretty as any
bride ever looked. She is smiling at George, who has
been slowly taking in the whole set-up. Through a
door he sees the end of a cheap bed, over the back
of which is a pair of pajamas and a nightie.

ERNIE
Master, if you want me, just ring.

Ernie exits and closes door. George looks at Mary.
Without taking her eyes off him, she turns off
phonograph.

GEORGE
(overcome)
Mary!

They rush into each other's arms, and hold each other
in ecstacy.

A male duet starts singing "Oh Promise Me."

Ernie and Bert, the cop, standing in the rain outside
window, singing.

BACK TO George and Mary. They remain embraced.

GEORGE
Mary, how -

> MARY
>
> I cashed in our railroad tickets.
> You're not too angry? Remember the
> night we threw rocks at this old
> house? This was what I wished for -

> GEORGE
>
> Darling, you're wonderful - just
> wonderful - just wonderful.

Their lips meet. "Oh Promise Me" continues.

DISSOLVE

CLARENCE AND JOSEPH - Clarence is continuing the last
few bars of "Oh Promise Me." Joseph looks at him
with infinite boredom.

> CLARENCE
>
> They sang that at my wedding, you know.
> (CHECK DATE OF SONG TO SEE IF THAT OLD)
> I was so excited I tried to put the
> ring on Parson Tuttle's finger -
> my wife said I never got over it.
> What a honeymoon we had!

> JOSEPH
>
> Must have made history.

> CLARENCE
>
> Just like George wanted to go away
> to build things I wanted to go away
> to study music, but my wife - she wore
> the pants you know - she says, "Clarence
> you get to work in my father's clock
> shop." And you know what?

> JOSEPH
>
> Couldn't guess.

> CLARENCE
>
> I went to work in her father's clock
> shop. And you know what else?

> JOSEPH
>
> I'm not very bright.

> CLARENCE
>
> I hated 'em. Tick tock - tick tock -
> tick tock. I hated 'em just like George
> hated what he was doing. But I conquered
> it believe me. You see I put my musical
> soul right into those confounded clocks.
> You know, the chimes -

                    CLARENCE (cont'd)
          (musically)
     Ding dong - ding dong. Yeah, that
     was me, you see. Today all over the
     world my chimes are ringing. Ding
     dong - ding dong! Ding dong - ding
     dong!

                    JOSEPH
     Hate to bring up clocks, but it's
     ten twenty.

                    CLARENCE
     yes, yes, knuckle down to work,
     of course. What's next?

                                        DISSOLVE

EXT. STREET - POTTERSFIELD - DAY - MED. SHOT

In front of one of the miserable shacks that line the
street are two vehicles. One of them is George Bailey's
rickety car, and directly behind it, in front of a
shack, is an even more rickety truck piled high with
household goods. The Martini family is moving. The
family consists of Martini, his wife and four kids
of various ages, from two to ten. George and Mary are
helping the Martinis move. About a dozen neighbors
crowd around. Martini and George, assisted by three
of the Martini children, are carrying out the last
of the furniture. As they emerge from the house
Martini calls out:

                    MARTINI
     Maria! Maria!
          (to the three kids)
     You! - Rosi, Teresa, Luccia, Mariano,
     hurry up! Don't you want to see the
     new house?

One of the neighbors, Schultz, cuts in:

                    SCHULTZ
     Martini, you really rented a new house?

                    MARTINI
          (in high spirits)
     Rent? Ha ha! Listen to him, Mr. Bailey -
          (to Schultz)
     I own the house. Me, Giuseppe Martini,
     I own my own house. the paint you still
     smell. No more we live like pigs in
     thisa Potter's Field. Hurry up!

                                        (CONTINUED)

(CONTINUED) 114

MRS. MARTINI
(coming out with an
armful, with Mary)
Madre mia, this is like a dream -
I'm so glad to leave this place -
(she gives a vigorous
spit toward house)
That for you, Mr. Potter!

MARTINI
That's nothing. You should see what
I -- never mind.

There is an appreciative howl from the neighbors.

GEORGE
(to Martini)
We'll take the kids in our car.

MARTINI
Thank you - thank you!

George takes the baby from Mrs. Martini and followed
by the three older children they go toward his car
and clamber in, while at the same time Martini and
his wife get into the truck. There is an ad lib of
exchanges between the Martinis and their neighbors.
George hands over the Martini baby to Mary as he
takes his seat at the wheel. He blows his horn to
indicate to Martini that he's ready and gets a blast
of horn in return.

MARTINI
Goodbye everybody!

NEIGHBORS
Goodbye!
Good luck!
Don't forget your old friends!
Etc.

ANOTHER ANGLE featureing the neighbors as they wave
and call "Goodbye!" to the Martinis. CAMERA PANS OVER
to a nearby sign:

NO TRESPASSING
Violators will be prosecuted
to the full extent of the law
HENRY F. POTTER

DISSOLVE

EXT. BAILEY PARK

CLOSE SHOT - Billboard sign. It reads:

                WELCOME TO BAILEY PARK

CAMERA PANS TOWARD street as a big black town car, a
block long and chauffeur driven, comes down the stret.
Bailey Park is a district of new small houses, not
all alike, but each individual. New lawns here and
there, and young trees. It has the promise when built
up of being a pleasant little middle class section.
As the big black car passes camera:

CLOSES MOVING SHOT - the black car. In it are seated
Sam Wainwright and his new wife. Sam is the epitome
of the successful, up and coming businessman. The new
Mrs. Wainwright is a very attractive, sophisticated
looking lady, dripping with furs and jewels. Sam,
looking out the window of his car, sees something o.s.
and he addresses an order to the chauffeur.

                         SAM
                    (to chauffeur)
               Stop a minute.

The car comes to a stop. Mrs. Wainwright follows
Sam's interested eyes to:

EXT. NEW HOUSE

MED. SHOT. The rickety truck and George's car are
parked in front. The truck is empty; all the furniture
has been moved into the house. A crowd of neighbors
is gathered in front.

INT. SAM'S CAR

TWO SHOT - Sam and his wife. Their attention is focused
upon:

EXT. NEW HOUSE AT ENTRANCE

MED. CLOSE SHOT. Mary is lining up the Martini family
in some kind of order to march toward the door. They
are speechless with joy. Martini keeps mumbling to
the group of neighbors about him: "Happy days, happy
days."

                         GEORGE
               Mr. and Mrs. Martini, welcome home!

                                        (CONTINUED)

The Martinis cross themselves. Crowd applauds.

                    GEORGE (cont'd)
          These four walls you see
          Will now your castle be;
          Where even kings must knock
          Before you turn the lock.
          But if to love and friends
          The welcome mat is out,
          Then heaven smiles, my friends,
          And all the angels shout.

The Martinis cross themselves again, almost in tears.
Mary takes up the ceremony.

                    SAM WAINWRIGHT
                    (o.s.)
          Hee, haw!

                    GEORGE
          Sam Wainwright!

                    MARY
                    (giving loaf of bread
                     to Mrs. Martini)
          Who cares! Bread! That this
          house may never see hunger.

Mrs. Martini crosses herself.

                    MARY (cont'd)
          Salt!
                    (she takes salt from
                     George and gives it
                     to Mrs. Martini)
          That life here may never lose its
          flavor!

                    GEORGE
          And wine!
                    (gives Martini bottle of wine)
          That joy and propserity may reign forever.

A cheer goes up from crowd. The Martinis are in tears.

                    GEORGE
                    (with a sweeping
                     gesture)
          Enter the Martini castle!

                              (CONTINUED)

The Martinis cross threshold, shaking hands all
around. The kids enter with screams of delight.
Mrs. Martini kisses Mary.

                    MRS. MARTINI
          A, Dio Mio - Dio Mio!

                    MARTINI
          Thank God, everybody! Thanks God!
          I'm lika king! Tonight I make
          everybody spaghetti - come in,
          please everybody! Thanks God!

As they disappear into the house we hear the stentorian
voice of Sam Wainwright.

                    SAM'S VOICE
          There's old George, now.
               (derisively)
          Hee-haw!

George and Mary look up and spot the parked car at
the curb off scene. Mary's reaction is friendly and
pleased; George seems taken aback and sheepish.

                    MARY
          Sam Wainwright!

She starts OUT OF SHOT, followed by George. CAMERA
PANS them over to the car. Sam opens the door of the
car as they come over and offers hearty greetings in
his usual ebullient style.

                    SAM
          Mary! George! What'cha doing,
          playing house? What is that voodoo
          stuff, George?

                    GEORGE
               (embarrassed)
          Nothing, Sam. just a gag - just a gag.

His eyes are on the magnificantly attired lady with
Sam.

                    SAM
          The new wife, George. De luxe, eh what?
               (to Mrs. Wainwright)
          Jane, these are a couple of urchins I
          grew up with -- George and Mary Bailiofski.

                                        (CONTINUED)

                    JANE
               (friendly)
          How do you do?

                    MARY
          Pleased to meet you.

                    GEORGE

          Hello, Jane. You're even
          prettier than Sam said --

                    SAM
               (kidding)
          Now, take it easy. You already
          took one girl away from me.
               (digs George
                in the ribs)
          Old George Casanova Bailey.

George's grin is forced and awkward. Mary senses his
mood, quickly changes the subject.

                    MARY
          It's good to see you, Sam. Will
          you and Jane have dinner with us
          tonight?

                    SAM
          Wish we could, honey - some other time.
          We just dropped in to see the new
          factory, then we're off to Florida.

                    JANE
               (brilliant notion)
          Why don't you ask your friends to come
          down with us?

                    SAM
          Yes, say, how's about you two coming
          down with us?

                    GEORGE
               (hollowly)
          I don't think I could hardly get away,
          Sam.

                    SAM
          Well, that's what you get for not coming
          in with me.
               (to Jane)
          I offered to let him in on the ground floor
          in plastics and he turned me down cold.

                              (CONTINUED)

                         GEORGE
          Don't rub it in, Sam.

                          SAM
          Okay, but the next time I ccme up
          with a proposition you better snap
          it up.
                    (puts his hand on
                     the door)
          Well, so long, folks, got to be
          shoving along.

There is handshaking all around and an interchange
of polite, "Glad to have seen you," etc., etc. Sam
closes the door of his car and the big limousine
glides away with Sam turning to wave farewell. "So
long. See you in the funny papers." "So long, Sam,
thanks for dropping around."

CLOSE SHOT - George and Mary. Mary sense that
George's mood is dour and unhappy as he looks after
the resplendent car. He takes her arm and they move
over to where his car is parked. He stares at the
tinny old vehicle broodingly.

                        GEORGE
          One of these days I'm going to get us
          a new car.

                         MARY
          Well, you're not going to turn this one
          in.

                        GEORGE
              (glares at her)
          Why not?

                         MARY
          I love this little old car.

                        GEORGE
          It's not a car, it's an ash can.

                         MARY
          It is not.

                        GEORGE
          It is so.

It looks like the beginning of quite a quarrel, but
there's an interruption as Cousin Eustice drives up
behind them on a bicycle.

                                    (CONTINUED)

                         EUSTICE
          George! George! Potter just phoned.
          He wants you down at the office.

                         GEORGE
          What's he want?

                         EUSTICE
          I don't know, but it's nothing trivial.
               (as car sputters)
          Need a tow?

                         GEORGE
          I don't know - tell you in a minute.

                         EUSTICE
          Better take the bike.

The car drives off.

CLOSE SHOT - George and Mary.

                         MARY
          I wonder what he wants to see you
          about.

                         GEORGE
          Whatever it is, it's bad news.

He presses the starter. The car asthmatically leaps
to life with a shudder, and as it jerks OUT OF SHOT

                         DISSOLVE TO:

INT. POTTER'S OFFICE

Lester Reineman, Potter's real estate man is standing
at Potter's desk with maps and photographs. He is
a gabby, straight-talking rent collector.

                         REINEMAN
          Look, Mr. Potter - it's no skin off
          my nose. I'm just your little rent
          collector. But you can't laugh this
          Bailey Park off any more.
               (unfolds map)
          Look at it.

                         POTTER
               (into inter-
                office phone)
          Tell the Congressman to wait.

                                    (CONTINUED)

                         REINEMAN
          Fifteen years ago a half-dozen houses
          were stuck here and there. There was
          the old cemetary - squirrels, buttercups,
          daisies - I shot rabbits there myself.
          Look at it today.
                    (unfolds another map)
          Dozens of the prettiest little houses
          you ever saw. Ninety percent owned by
          suckers who used to pay rent to you!
          Your Potter's Field, my dear Mr.
          Employer, is becoming just that. And
          the local yokels making wise with those
          David and Goliath wisecracks.

                         POTTER
                    (burning)
          Is that so? Even though the
          Baileys haven't made a dime out of it.

                         REINEMAN
          You know very well why - the
          Baileys are chumps. Every one of those
          new homes is worth twice what it cost
          the Building and Loan to build them.
          If I were you, Mr. Potter -

                         POTTER
                    (pressing button)
          Well, you aren't me.

Reineman folds his maps.

                         REINEMAN
          Well, as I say, it's no skin off
          my nose -
                    (goes to door)
          - except one of these days this
          bright young man is going to ask
          George Bailey for a job.

He exits.

                         POTTER
          The Bailey family has been a boil on
          my neck long enough -
                    (to secretary on
                     inter-office phone)
          Come in here.

                                        DISSOLVE TO:

                                        (CONTINUED)

(CONTINUED)

INT. POTTER'S OFFICE -

CLOSEUP. George, a big cigar in his mouth. Potter's
hand holding a lighter.

                    GEORGE
          Thanks. Quite a cigar, Mr. Potter.

MED. SHOT - George and Potter.

                    POTTER
          Like it? I'll send you a box.

                    GEORGE
          Well - suppose you'll tell me sooner
          or later -- but what exactly did you
          want to see me about?

                    POTTER
               (pleasantly and smooth)
          George, that's just what I like about
          you. I might as well get to the point --
          lay my cards right out on the table --
          you know me too well. Besides, George,
          you're too smart to talk to any other
          way. George, I'm an old man, and most
          people hate me. But I don't like them
          either, so that makes it all even. I ask
          no quarter, and I give none. And, you
          know as well as I do that I run practically
          everything in town, but the Bailey Building
          and Loan. And you also know that for years
          I've tried to get control of it or to kill
          it. But, I haven't been able to do it.
          You've been stopping me. In fact, you've
          beaten me, George - and as anybody in
          this county can tell you, that takes some
          doing. Take during the depression for
          instance. You and I were the only ones
          that kept our heads. You saved the
          Building and Loan and I saved all the
          rest.

                    GEORGE
          Most people say you stole all the rest.

                    POTTER
          The envious ones say that, George - the
          suckers. You and I know it was just good
          business on my part. Now, to get back:
          When I lose a case in court, I try to hire
          the other lawyer. My theory is, if you
          can't beat 'em, join 'em.

                              (CONTINUED)

                         GEORGE
                    (rising)
          Are you suggesting --

                         POTTER
          Now wait, George, sit down. You're
          going to make a very important
          decision here - probably the most
          important decision of your life -
          so take it easy, son. Now. I've told
          my side, frankly young man. Let's look at
          your side. Young man, twenty-seven,
          twenty-eight - married, making say -
          forty a week.

                         GEORGE
          Forty-five.

                         POTTER
          Forty-five. Out of which, after
          supporting your mother and paying the
          bills, you keep - maybe - ten, if you
          skimp. Maybe a child or two will come
          along and you won't even save the ten.
          Now if this young man of twenty-eight
          was a common, ordinary yokel, I'd say
          he was doing fine. But - George Bailey
          is not a common, ordinary yokel. He's
          an intelligent, smart, ambitious young
          man - who hates his job - who hates the
          Building and Lona, almost as much as I
          do. A young man who's been dying to get
          out on his own ever since he was born.
          A young man who sits by and watches his
          friends go places -- while he's trapped -
          yes, trapped into frittering away his
          life playing nursemaid to a lot of
          garlic eaters. A young man who's much
          worse off than any of the riff-raff he
          builds such nice houses for. Do I paint
          a correct picture, or do I exaggerate?

                         GEORGE
          What's your point, Mr. Potter?

                         POTTER
          Point? Point is, I want to hire you.

                         GEORGE
          Hire me!

                                   (CONTINUED)

                        POTTER
          Manage my affairs, run my properties.
          I'll start you at twenty thousand
          a year.

George drops his cigar on his lap. He nervously
brushes off the sparks from his clothes.

                        GEORGE
          Twenty thousand?

                        POTTER
          You wouldn't mind living in the best
          house in town - getting your wife
          some fine clothes - New York on business
          a couple of times a year - once in a
          while to Europe - would you, George.

                        GEORGE
          Would I?
                  (looking around
                   him skeptically)
          You're not talking to somebody else,
          are you? This is me - remember me?
          George Bailey.

                        POTTER
          Yes, George Bailey. A young man whose
          ship has just come in, providing he
          has brains enough to come aboard.

                        GEORGE
          What about the Building and Loan?

                        POTTER
          Building and Loan? What about it? It's
          you I want, not the Building and Loan.
              (throwing it off)
          With you gone it'll probably -- collapse.
          So what? At twenty thousand a year you'll
          stop worrying about the other side of the
          tracks.

                        GEORGE
          Yeah, yeah. Twenty thousand a year!
          Twenty thousand!

                        POTTER
          Is it a deal?

                                        (CONTINUED)

                    GEORGE
I know I'm a fool, Mr. Potter -- but
if I'm such a misfit, according to
the record, why do you, the biggest man
in the county, want to <u>hire</u> me?

                    POTTER
Why? Because until you get some money
of your own, you'll always be one of
those blasted little men with tough
convictions. The kind that hasn't got
sense enough to get out of the way. I
had the same trouble with your father.
Now, George, I don't want you to get in
the way -- that's why I want to hire you.
Understand.

                    GEORGE
Get in the way of what, Mr. Potter?

                    POTTER
Confound it man, are you afraid of
success? I'm offering you a three-year
contract at twenty thousand a year,
starting today. Is it a deal, or isn't
it?

                    GEORGE
        (stands up)
I - I - I know I should jump at this,
Mr. Potter. Could you give me twenty-
four hours to think it over?

                    POTTER
Sure, sure, son. Talk it over with your
wife.

                    GEORGE
Gee, I'd like that.

                    POTTER
Meantime, I'll draw up the papers.
        (offers hand)
Okay, George?

                    GEORGE
        (taking his
         hand)
Okay, Mr. Potter.

                                        (CONTINUED)

As they shake hands, George feels a physical revulsion.
Potter's hand feels like a cold mackeral to him. In
that moment of physical contact he knows he could never
be associated with this man. George drops his hand
with a shudder. He peers intently into Potter's face.

GEORGE

I don't need twenty-four hours.
I don't have to talk to anyone.
I know right now. The answer is
no! No! If you offered me a
million to stay in this town and
play stooge for you, the answer
would still be no.
> (getting madder
> all the time)

You sit here and spin your webs
and think the whole world revolves
around you and your money. Well,
it doesn't, Mr. Potter. In the vast
configuration of things I'd say you
were nothing but a scurvy little
spider.
> (to goon)

And you, too!
> (at door to
> secretary)

And it goes for you, too!

George turns and goes out door.

POTTER

> (livid)

You're going to eat those words,
George Bailey.

NOTE: These
two speeches
shot
alternately in
and out

Reineman steps into office from adjoining room. He
has evidently been listening. Potter rings for his
secretary.

REINEMAN

He's not just a boil on your neck.
He's going to be a carbuncle.

The secretary enters.

POTTER

> (to secretary)

First thing every morning, I want
you to say to me, "George Bailey."
That's all -- "George Bailey."

SECRETARY

Yes, Mr. Potter.

DISSOLVE OUT

INT. GEORGE'S CAR (IN MOTION) - NIGHT - (PROCESS B.G.)

CLOSE SHOT - George is at the wheel, driving home.
The expression on his face indicates that he is in
a mood of complete frustration. We get a clue to
his thoughts from the eerie jumble of voices which
come into shot.

                    POTTER'S VOICE
          George Bailey is not a common ordinary
          yokel. He's an intelligent, smart,
          ambitious young man.

                    SAM'S VOICE
          Hee- haw! Hee- haw!

                    MRS. MARTINI'S VOICE
          Dio mio! -- Dio mio!

                    POTTER'S VOICE
          Trapped -- trapped, into frittering away
          his life, playing nursemaid to a lot of
          garlic-eaters.

                    MARTINI'S VOICE
          Ha-ha, I own my own house!

                    POTTER'S VOICE
          Young man who's much worse off than the
          riffraff he builds such nice houses for.

                    MARTINI'S VOICE
          Thanks, God! Thanks, God! I'm like a
          king!

                    POTTER'S VOICE
          Young man, twenty- seven, twenty-eight --
          married, making say -- forty a week.
               (continues like
                a broken record)
          Forty a week -- forty a week --
          forty a week --

                    SAM'S VOICE
          Plastics from soy beans.

                    MRS. MARTINI'S VOICE
          Dio mio!

                    MARTINI'S VOICE
          Thanks, God!

                                        (CONTINUED)

                         POTTER'S VOICE
          Forty a week!

The car pulls up to the curb in front of George's house.

EXT. CAR

CLOSE SHOT. George gets out of the car. CAMERA TRUCKS
BEFORE him as he walks slowly to the gate.

                         SAM'S VOICE
          I don't forget my old friends. Got any
          money?

                         POTTER'S VOICE
          Forty a week.

                         SAM'S VOICE
          I'm letting you in on the ground floor.
          A chance of a lifetime.

                         MARY'S VOICE
          The chance of a lifetime.

CLOSEUP - George at gate.

                         SAM'S VOICE
          We just dropped off to see the factory,
          then we're off to Florida - Florida -
          Florida - Florida.

                         MARY'S VOICE
          If you want to spend the rest of your
          life building a bridge to the moon,
          that's your business.

                         HIS FATHER'S VOICE
          You've got talent, son, don't stick
          around here and be a failure like me.

                         POTTER'S VOICE
          You wouldn't mind living in the best
          house in town.

REVERSE ANGLE - FULL - SHOT - (SHOOTING FROM behind
George's back).

                         POTTER'S VOICE
          The best house in town.

                                              (CONTINUED)

CLOSE SHOT - at gate.

>   POTTER'S VOICE
>   Getting your wife some fine clothes --

George opens the gate and slowly starts toward the
house, CAMERA TRUCKING BEFORE him.

>   POTTER'S VOICE
>   New York on business a couple times
>   a year -- once in a while to Europe --

George reaches the steps, starts to mount them.

>   POTTER'S VOICE (cont'd)
>   Now wait, George, sit down.

George sits on steps, reaches down into the roadway,
picks up some gravel and starts tossing it, fragment
by fragment, into the shrubbery.

>   POTTER'S VOICE (cont'd)
>   You're going to make a very important
>   decsiion here.

George looks up at:

SKY SHOT - The moon is lovely and luminous.

>   POTTER'S VOICE
>   (reiterating
>   doggedly)
>   Very important - very important -
>   very important - very important -

CLOSE SHOT - George.

>   POTTER'S VOICE
>   I'll start you at twenty thousand a
>   year -- you wouldn't mind living in
>   the best house in town - New York,
>   Europe. If you can't beat 'em, join
>   'em. Join 'em - join 'em - join 'em --

From within the house comes the measured bonging of a
clock. George shakes his head, gets up, goes to the
door, lets himself in with his key.

INT. LIVING ROOM - NIGHT

FULL SHOT - A table lamp has been left lit for George.
The house has been partly fixed up since we last saw
it. Curtains are up and a cheap rug is on the floor.
The furniture is modest and obviously temporary.
George looks bleakly about. CAMERA MOVES UP TOWARD
one wall of the room, where a plank has been set on
two chairs for a scaffolding, a paste bucket and rolls
of wallpaper are on the floor, half of the room has
been papered with a new and colorful design of wall
paper. From the balance of the wall the old wallpaper
has been torn off. Mary's smock has been draped across
the scaffolding.

As CAMERA MOVES CLOSER, the figure of Mary DISSOLVES
INTO SHOT, dressed in her smock, standing on the
scaffolding, putting on the new wallpaper.

CLOSEUP - George, watching.

TRICK PAN SHOT.

CAMERA MOVES ABOUT the room and wherever it goes it
PICKS UP Mary. She is at a sewing machine, sewing
on curtains; she is on a chair, hanging the curtains;
she is crouched down, varnishing a table; she is on
her knees, mopping the floor; she is arranging flowers
in a vase - hydrangeas.

INT. ROOM

FULL SHOT. THE ROOM IS EMPTY, AS BEFORE.

CLOSE SHOT - George. His attention is attracted by
a sign propped up in a section of the room which
commands a view of both hallway and dining room. George
walks over to the sign to look at it. The sign is
on cardboard with crayon lettering. It reads:

> IF YOU'RE HUNGRY
> (with an arrow
> pointing to
> dining room)

> IF YOU'RE NOT
> (with an arrow
> pointing to hallway)

INSERT TOP PORTION OF SIGN

> IF YOU'RE HUNGRY
> (arrow pointing
> to dining room)

CLOSE SHOT - George. His eyes follow the arrow to:

SHOT of dining room - George's ANGLE.

A snack with coffee in thermos bottle has been set
up for George.

INT. LIVING ROOM

CLOSE SHOT - George. He looks at the lower half of
sign.

INSERT   LOWER HALF OF SIGN

               IF YOU'RE NOT
                    (arrow points
                     to stairway
                     in hall)

INT. LIVING ROOM

MED. SHOT. George isn't hungry. He exits to hallway.

INT.   HALLWAY

FULL SHOT. George starts up the stairway toward the
living quarters upstairs. We see him pause before the
bedroom door, hestitate, then as he opens it:

INT. BEDROOM

FULL SHOT. The room is lit only by moonlight, as
George enters. He stands looking long at the bed.

CLOSE SHOT - at bed. Mary is asleep, her face lovely
in the moonlight.

INT. ROOM

FULL SHOT. Carefully, so as not to wake Mary, George
starts to undress. He takes off his coat and vest,
drapes them over a chair, and then turns to the dresser:

INT. BEDROOM

(CONTINUED)

Mary suddenly starts singing "Buffalo Gal" in bed.
George crosses to her and sits on bed. They clinch.

                    GEORGE
          Hi.

                    MARY
          Hi.

                    GEORGE
          Mary Hatch! Why in the world did
          you ever marry a guy like me?

                    MARY
          To keep from being an old maid.

                    GEORGE
          You could have married Sam Wainwright --
          anybody else in town.

                    MARY
          I didn't want to marry anybody else
          in town. I wanted my baby to look
          like you.

                    GEORGE
          You didn't even have a honeymoon.
          I promised --
               (does a take)
          You what- ?

                    MARY
          A baby.

                    GEORGE
          You mean you're on the nest.

They kiss.

                    MARY
          George Bailey lassoes the stork.

                                   FADE OUT

DISSOLVE IN

Clarence and Joseph. Clarence is blowing his nose.
Tears come down his face. Joseph looks at him in
disgust.

                              (CONTINUED)

                              JOSEPH
          What's the matter with you?
          It's George who's in trouble, not you.

Official comes in and listens to rest of scene.

                              CLARENCE
          Never mind me. I -- I always cry
          when other people are happy. Show me
          some more.

                              JOSEPH
          If that's what it does to you,
          maybe I better tell you what
          happened. Listen closely, Huck
          Finn. Now, you've probably already
          guessed that George never gets out
          of Bedford Falls.

                              CLARENCE
                    (dismayed)
          No!

                              JOSEPH
          Yes. Mary had her child - a boy.
          Then she had another one - a girl.
          Potter made it tough for George, but
          he struggles along, still dreaming and
          hoping. Then came the war, the best and
          finest war they ever had. Mrs. Bailey
          and Mrs. Hatch joined the Red Cross and
          sewed. Mary ran the USO and had two
          more babies. Sam Wainwright made a
          fortune in plastic hoods for planes.
          Potter became head of the draft board
          and paid the biggest income tax in his
          part of the state. Violet Bick joined
          the Waves until they found out her kind
          of morale building would sink the Navy.
          Gower and Uncle Billy sold war bonds.
          Bert the Cop was wounded in North Africa--
          got a silver star. Ernie the Taxi-driver
          was captured, escaped and came back
          through Russia. Marty helped capture
          Remagen Bridge across the Rhine. Harry -
          Harry Bailey topped them all. A Navy
          flier, he shot down fifteen planes -
          two of them as they were about to crash
          into a transport full of soldiers.

                                        (CONTINUED)

                            CLARENCE
          Yes, but George - what happened to George?

                            JOSEPH
          George? George just kept getting older.
          4-F on account of his ear, he worked like
          mad around town. OPA clerk, air raid
          warden, scrap drives, paper drives,
          rubber drives. His office looked like a
          junk yard. Wrote every day to his friends
          and brother. At night he'd read their
          answers and set out their adventures for
          his kids. Like everybody else, on V-E day
          he wept and prayed again.

                            CLARENCE
          What about his dreams? What about the
          Building and Loan? What about Potter?

                            OFFICIAL
                       (Ben Franklin)
          Show him the climax - what happened
          today. Only a few minutes left.

                            JOSEPH
                       (starting machine
                        again)
          Yes, sir.
                       (to Clarence)
          This morning, day before Christmas
          -- about ten A.M., Bedford Falls time --

MED. SHOT - SHOOTING TOWARD SCREEN - CAMERA MOVES UP TO:

EXT. MAIN STREET - BEDFORD FALLS - DAY

CLOSE (MOVING SHOT) - A copy of the Bedford Falls Herald
held in a man's hands. The MOVING CAMERA PEEPS OVER the
man's shoulder and with him takes in a story featured
with an eight-column line, reading:

     CITY TO CELEBRATE HERO'S HOMECOMING!

George, Ernie and Gower on street corner. Other people,
congratulating.

                            AD LIBS
          Extra! Extra!
          Snow again!
          What do you mean snow - look at
          the headlines - Comdr Harry Bailey -
          Wonderful - Look at this -
          Maybe I should have joined the Navy!

The sub-head tells of a plan for a giant jubilee and
parade, to be followed by a banquet, in honor of
Commander Harry Bailey, U.S.N. on his way home from
Washington after receiving the Congressional Medal
of Honor. There's a large picture of President Truman
pinning the coveted medal on Harry's bosom, in the
midst of dignitaries; a picture of the destroyer which
Harry saved, together with the entire crew; a solo
picture of Harry, smiling. Practically the whole front
page is devoted to the story.

REVERSE ANGLE (MOVING CAMERA). The paper is being
read by George, who is jay-walking across the street.
It's a raw, gusty day. His overcoat and muffler flap
in the breeze. Draped around one arm is a large
Christmas wreath. Under his other arm are several
more copies of the paper. His lips move inaudibly
as he reads the details of the projected celebration.
He's completely oblivious of passing traffic. He
passes somebody who is jay-walking across the street
in the opposite direction. It's Uncle Billy. Both
men are so preoccupied that neither one sees the other.

CLOSE (MOVING) SHOT - Uncle Billy. His glasses are
over his forehead as he moves across the street,
narrowly missing death by traffic. He is mumbling
under his breath, tallying something off on his fingers.
At the same time receives congratulations from passersby
"Wonderful about Harry," "I've seen it already."

                         UNCLE BILLY
                    (muttering)
               Shall for Mary...Mrs.Hatch...Ties
               for George...Sled for Pete...

EXT. BUILDING & LOAN ASSOCIATION BUILDING - DAY

MED. SHOT. Still reading the newspaper, George enters
the building.

EXT. BAND BUILDING ACROSS THE STREET - DAY

MED. SHOT. Still engaged in mental Christmas shopping
Uncle Billy goes into the revolving door of the bank.
He makes a complete turn, emerges into the street,
and continues on.

                         UNCLE BILLY
               Then there's Jane...Skates...Zuzu...

                                          (CONTINUED)

He stops and gazes blankly about. He shakes his head
ruefully at the realization of his absent-mindedness,
then he goes into the revolving door and this time
he enters the bank.

INT. BANK - DEPOSIT SLIP DESK

CLOSE SHOT. Uncle Billy is ready to make out a
deposit slip, but he can't find his glasses. He thumbs
his various pockets.

                    UNCLE BILLY
          Now where in tarnation --

He raises his hand to scratch his head in vexed
perplexity. His hand encounters the edge of the
glasses and with a sigh of relief he pulls them over
his eyes. From his inside coat pocket he takes out
a fat envelope and places it on the desk before him.
In the envelope we get a glimpse of greenbacks.
Apparently it is a substantial deposit he's about to
make. As he starts to fill out the deposit blank:

MED. SHOT. Potter is being wheeled into the bank. He
is absorbed in reading paper. Uncle Billy sees him
and can't help taking advantage of it.

                    UNCLE BILLY
               (overly friendly)
          Good morning, Mr.Potter.
          What's the news? What's the news:
          Haven't seen a paper in a week.
               (he takes paper from
                Potter's hands and reads.
                Potter is coldly furious)
          Well, well, well, well! "Harry
          Bailey wins Congressional Medal."
          Couldn't be one of the Bailey boys?
          Well, you just can't keep those
          Bailey's down, can you, Mr. Potter?

                    POTTER
          What does slacker George think about
          that - Harry being decorated?

                    UNCLE BILLY
          Very jealous. Very jealous.
          George only lost three buttons off his
          vest.

He folds paper over money envelop and looks for his
deposit slip.

                                        (CONTINUED)

                         UNCLE BILLY (cont'd)
Of course if slacker George had gone, he
would have brought back <u>two</u> of those
medals.

                         POTTER
Oh yes, yes, bad ear. Hears everything
out of it but the call to arms though.

                         UNCLE BILLY
               (handing back the folded
                paper to Potter. Inside the
                paper is the money envelope)
After all, Potter, we had to keep some
people like George to stay home - because
not <u>all</u> the heels were in Germany and Japan,
you know.

In a cold rage Potter grabs his paper and wheels off
toward his office. Uncle Billy smiles triumphantly
and goes toward deposit window with his deposit slip.

                         TELLER
Morning, Uncle Billy.

                         UNCLE BILLY
Morning, Horace.

He hands the bank book over. The teller opens it,
starts to punch it with rubber stamps.

                         TELLER
Looks like we've got a white Xmas for
Harry's homecoming!

                         UNCLE BILLY
Yes, yes.
     (waits)

                         TELLER
     (smiles)
Guess you forgot something.

                         UNCLE BILLY
Huh?

                         TELLER
You forgot something.

                         UNCLE BILLY
What?

                                        (CONTINUED)

                              TELLER
            Aren't you making a deposit?

                           UNCLE BILLY
            Sure I am.

                              TELLER
            Well, then -

The people back of Uncle Billy start to snicker and
exchange glances. Apparently they're not unfamiliar
with the old man's vagaries.

                        TELLER (cont'd)
                 (winks at the line)
            It's usually customary to bring the
            money along with you.

                           UNCLE BILLY
            Shucks.
                 (looks bewildered)
            Excuse me.

                              TELLER
                 (indicates string)
            Try the little finger
                 (as Uncle Billy walks
                  away to next man in line)
            Uncle Billy's getting more absent-
            minded every day.

                               MAN
            He certainly is.

He steps out of line. CAMERA PANS him BACK TO the
deposit slip desk.

CLOSE SHOT - deposit slip desk. Uncle Billy looks
around for the money envelope. It's not there. He
looks puzzled, thinks hard, then a look of concern
creeps into his eyes. He starts thumbing his pockets,
with increasing panic. His search becomes so frantic
that he begins to look, for all the world, like a man
with St. Vitus dance.

INT. POTTER'S OFFICE

Potter has taken his coat and hat off and is about to
sit down when Uncle Billy's envelop with the money
slips out of newspaper. Potter picks it up - sees it
is full of money - realizes what has happened. He goes
to door to peek out. He sees Uncle Billy frantically
searching himself and then run out of bank. A diabolical
smile crosses over Potter's face. He goes to dictaphone
and buzzes.

                                        (CONTINUED)

                        O'NEIL'S VOICE
          Yes, sir.

                        POTTER
          O'Neil, did the bank examiner finish
          here yesterday?

                        O'NEIL'S VOICE
          Yes, sir. He's over at the Building and
          Loan this morning. Want him?

                        POTTER
          No, thank you.
               (to goon)
          Hang up my hat!

Potter's secretary comes in. Potter slips money
envelope into a drawer. As has been her wont for
years, she says in an oft-repeated sing-song fashion:

                        MISS LESTER
          George Bailey. George Bailey.

                        POTTER
          Yes, George Bailey.

                        MISS LESTER
          How much longer do I have to say to
          you every day, "George Bailey?"

                        POTTER
          Miss Lester, as a little Xmas present,
          you may stop from now on.

                        MISS LESTER
          Oh, good.

                        POTTER
          What's good about it.

                                        DISSOLVE OUT

INT. OUTER OFFICE - BUILDING & LOAN - DAY

Cousin Tilly on phone talking to Harry Bailey. Cousin
Eustace listening in. Carter, bank examiner,
impatiently sitting nearby. George comes in.

                        COUSIN TILLY
               (on phone)
          Yes, Harry, on the front lawn.

                                        (CONTINUED)

                          GEORGE
Extra! Extra!

                       COUSIN EUSTACE
George! George! It's Harry now -- on
long distance from Washington!

                       COUSIN TILLY
      (on phone)
Here he is now, Harry.

                       COUSIN EUSTACE
He reversed the charges. It's okay,
isn't it, George?

                          GEORGE
      (taking phone)
What do you mean it's okay -- for a
hero?
      (into phone)
Harry -- you old seven kinds of a so-and-
so -- congratulation! You did? How did
Mother take it?....She did?
      (aside to others)
Had lunch with the President's wife.

                          TILLY
Wait 'til Martha hears about this. What
did they have to eat?

                          GEORGE
      (into phone)
Well, wait 'til you see what the town's
cooking up for you....They are?
      (to others)
The Navy's flying them up this afternoon.

                       COUSIN EUSTACE
In a plane?

                          GEORGE
      (on phone)
Uncle Billy?
      (to others)
Uncle Billy come in yet?

                       COUSIN TILLY
Stopping at the bank first.

                          GEORGE
      (into phone)
He'll be right here, Harry. Now tell
me all about it.

                                       (CONTINUED)

                         EUSTACE
                  (whispering to
                   George secretly)
          George -- George -- that man's here
          again.
                  (indicates Carter)

                         GEORGE
                  (into   phone)
          Harry, talk to Cousin Tilly for a minute,
          I'll be right back.
                  (to Carter)
          Morning.

                         CARTER
          Carter -- bank examiner.

                         GEORGE
          That's my brother, you know. Medal of
          honor. The President decorated him this
          morning.

                         CARTER
                  (unimpressed)
          Well, I guess those things have to be.
          I trust you've had a good year.

                         GEORGE
          Just between you and me, we're broke.

                         CARTER
          Yes, very funny.

                         GEORGE
                  (ushers him into
                   small office)
          Right in here, Mr.Carter.

                         CARTER
          Now, if you'll cooperate, I'd like
          to finish with you by tonight.
          I want to spend Christmas in Elmira
          with my family.

                         GEORGE
          I don't blame you, Mr. Carter.
          We'll get the books ready for you.

                         TILLY
          Shall I hang up?

                                      (CONTINUED)

                        GEORGE
          Of course not. He wants to talk to
          Uncle Billy, too.

                        TILLY
               (into phone)
          It's all right, Harry, it won't
          take long to put the books in order
          and he'll be right with you.

Violet enters office and goes to George.

                        GEORGE
          Hello, Vi.

                        VIOLET
          Can I see you just a minute?

Uncle Billy comes in, harrassed and mumbling. Bird
flies to meet him at the door.

                        GEORGE
          Uncle Billy -- Harry's on the phone.
          Hurry up.

George and Violet go into his office. Uncle Billy, very
preoccupied, picks up phone.

                        UNCLE BILLY
               (into phone)
          Hello, Harry -- everything's just fine.
               (he absent-
                mindedly hangs
                up phone. Going
                towards his office)
          I should have my head examined.
          Eight thousand dollars! It's got to
          be some place.

Carter watches proceedings patiently from the door of
the small office.

INT. GEORGE'S OFFICE - FULL SHOT

George is typing out a letter. Violet stands back of
him, watching over his shoulder.

INSERT - THE LETTER

On the stationery of the Building & Loan Association
George has typed out the following:

               TO WHOM IT MAY CONCERN:

                                              (CONTINUED)

BACK TO SHOT

George looks up at Violet.

                    GEORGE
          What'll I say?

                    VIOLET
              (bitterly)
          Well, you might start by telling Mr. whom
          it might concern how the good city
          mothers boycotted me and practically ran
          me out of town.

                    GEORGE
          You're no help.

George frowns, thinks deeply, stares up at the ceiling
for inspiration, then starts banging away. Violet bends
over his shoulder to read.

INSERT: THE LETTER

The keys start typing:

          The bearer, Miss Violet Bick,
          has been employed as a clerk by
          this company for the past two years.

BACK TO SHOT

                    VIOLET
          That's a lie, George.

He continues typing. She reads over his shoulder.

INSERT: THE LETTER

George's fingers type out:

          The undersigned is glad to recommend
          her for

As the fingers hesitate:

CLOSEUP - VIOLET

Watching the keyboard.

                                        (CONTINUED)

INSERT: THE LETTER

The keys start typing out:

      intelligence,

                      VIOLET'S VOICE
      A lie.

The keys type out:

      ability,

                      VIOLET'S VOICE
      A lie.

The keys type out:

      and good character.

                      VIOLET'S VOICE
      That's a real lie.

BACK TO SHOT

                      GEORGE
         (sternly)
      Who's writing this letter?

                      VIOLET
      You are, George -- it's not about
      me -

                      GEORGE
      Don't worry, it's about you,
      all right. When are you going to leave?

                      VIOLET
      Right away.

                      GEORGE
      That's fine.

INSERT: THE LETTER

The keys type out the signature:

      BAILEY BUILDING & LOAN ASSOCIATION

                      President.

BACK TO SHOT

George jerks the sheet out of the roller, reaches for
a pen and signs with a bold, flamboyant gesture, as
if it were the Magna Carta.

> VIOLET
> Character? If I had any character
> I'd never be --

> GEORGE
> It takes character to leave your home
> town and start all over again. Here
> you are.

He takes out his wallet, extracts its contents -
three twenties - and inserts them into the envelope.

> VIOLET
> (her voice
> husky)
> No, George, don't -

> GEORGE
> You're broke, aren't you? What are
> you going to do -- hock your fur coat
> and your hat? How're you going to get
> to New York? Walk? And when you get
> there, then what? They charge for rent
> and meals in New York, too, you know.

> VIOLET
> I know, but --

> GEORGE
> It's a loan. That's my business, Vi,
> Building and Loan. You'll get a job --

He rises and hands her the envelope.

> GEORGE (cont'd)
> Good luck to you, Vi. I may see you
> up there.

He offers his hand. She takes it, then comes closer
to him.

> VIOLET
> Georgie-Porgie, why don't you come
> with me to New York? You don't like
> this town any more than I do.

He looks at her without answering. Her voice takes
on a note of seductive urgency.

(CONTINUED)

> VIOLET (cont'd)
> Sure, I know, you've got a wife and
> family, but you don't belong here.
> We could have a lot of fun together.
> Like you once said, remember? We'll
> go on an all-night binge, walk down
> Broadway in sandals, take a swim in
> that fountain at Radio City and watch
> the sun come up over the Empire State
> Building. What do you say? Are you
> game, Georgie-Porgie?

He says nothing, just looks at her without anger,
without criticism, pityingly. Suddenly she's weeping
against George's chest. Awkwardly he pats her on
the shoulder, more distressed than she is.

> VIOLET (cont'd)
> (sobbing)
> Just a -- just a little whistling
> in the dark --

> GEORGE
> Sure.

Her sobbing subsides. She looks up at him with a
twisted smile.

> VIOLET
> I'm glad I know you, George Bailey --
> Forget what I said, will you?

> GEORGE
> Merry Christmas, Vi. Say hello
> to New York for me.

> VIOLET
> Sure I will.

> GEORGE
> Let's hear from you once in a while.

She reaches up and kisses him on cheek, leaving
lipstick. George opens the door for her.

INT. OUTER OFFICE

Eustace, Tilly and bank examiner see George and Violet
come out of his office. She puts money in her purse.
They also see lipstick on George.

(CONTINUED)

                         VIOLET
                (wiping lipstick off
                 George's cheek)
            Merry Christmas, Georgie.

The office help react to this intimacy.

                      BANK EXAMINER
            Mr. Bailey, may I please have the
            books, cash and bank deposits?

                         GEORGE
            Sorry, of course. Forgot about you.
                (to Tilly)
            Uncle Billy in yet?

                         TILLY
            In his office.

                         GEORGE
                (to bank examiner)
            Be with you in a second.

George strides into Uncle Billy's office.

INT. DOORWAY - UNCLE BILLY'S OFFICE

MED. SHOT. George opens door. Uncle Billy is surprised,
taking a nip. He is dishevelled, drawers are open,
waste basket dumped out, etc.

                         GEORGE
                (in doorway)
            Hi, unk -- I need the accounts -- hey,
            what's going on in here? The bank
            examiner's here and I --
                (he closes door
                 behind him)

                         TILLY
                (on phone to Martha)
            Martha you should have seen them.
            She had money in her hand and he had
            lipstick all over him! They say she
            counts wolves in her sleep.

Eustace covers her mouth as George dashes out of
Uncle Billy's office.

                                        (CONTINUED)

154 MED. SHOT. George goes directly to safe and
starts searching. He doesn't find money.

> GEORGE
> Eustace, come here.
> (motions him over)
> Did you see Uncle Billy with any
> cash last night?

> EUSTACE
> Had it on his desk counting it
> when we closed up.

Carter (bank examiner) stands impatiently at his
office doorway.

(These four shots of Potter in his office at the
phone will (INTERCUT with the sequence concerning the
loss of the eight thousand dollars)

SHOT "A" POTTER AT PHONE.

> POTTER
> Hello...Carter? This is Potter talking...
> Merry Christmas...I understand you're
> looking over the books of the Building
> and Loan. Well now, I feel it's my duty
> as a director of the company --

SHOT "B" POTTER AT PHONE.

> POTTER
> Let me talk to the district attorney....
> Gill? This is Potter. Quite well, thank
> you. Just a rumor, but I thought you
> ought to know about it...

SHOT "C" POTTER AT PHONE.

> POTTER
> Let me talk to the city editor. That
> you, Flynn? Potter. Merry Christmas.
> Look, not that I know anything, but
> there's something phoney at the
> Building and Loan. Look, it wouldn't
> hurt to send a man over there....

> CARTER
> (annoyed)
> May I please have the books,
> cash and the bank deposits?

                        GEORGE
            Coming right up, Mr. Carter.
            Eustace, give him the books.

                        CARTER
            I have to finish here by tonight.
            Tomorrow is Christmas you know.

George goes back to Uncle Billy's office, and
closes door.

CLOSE SHOT. Ed and Miss Brackett. They know something
is radically wrong.

MED. SHOT. Suddenly George and Uncle Billy come rushing
out of Uncle Billy's office, Uncle Billy putting on
his hat and coat. They both fly out of the office
without paying attention to anybody.

CLOSEUP - Carter. Carter watches the hasty exit with
a suspicious look.

INT. POTTER'S OFFICE

Potter is at window looking out on street. He sees
something which attracts his attention.

EXT. BUILDING AND LOAN

George and Uncle Billy come out and head toward
Uncle Billy's house. George is scanning the sidewalk
and gutter as they go.

INT. POTTER OFFICE

Potter turns and smiles with satisfaction.

EXT. BEDFORD FALLS STREET - RESIDENTIAL DISTRICT

George and Uncle Billy looking for money.

                        GEORGE
            Did you buy anything?

                        UNCLE BILLY
            Not a stick of gum. Didn't talk
            to a soul.

                                        (CONTINUED)

                    GEORGE
          All right. We'll go over every
          step since you left the house --
          this way?

INT. UNCLE BILLY'S LIVING ROOM - NIGHT

CLOSE SHOT - an ancient coo-coo clock. It registers
six o'clock. The little door pops open, the coo-coo
bird comes out, and as it gives out with its six
calls: Coo-coo! Coo-coo! Coo-coo! Coo-coo! Coo-
coo! Coo-coo! CAMERA PULLS BACK to take in the
living room - a shabby, old-fashioned, gaslit room
which has been turned almost inside-out and upside-
down in an effort to locate the missing money.
Drawers of an old secretary have been pulled out
and are on the floor. Every conceivable place which
might have been used by Uncle Billy to put the money
has been searched. George, in his shirt-sleeves,
his hair rumpled, is feverishly pursuing the search,
as Uncle Billy comes in from the hall. George looks
at him tensely. The old man shakes his head.

                    BILLY
          Any luck?

                    GEORGE
          I've searched every foot of every street
          in Bedford Falls.

                    UNCLE BILLY
          It's no use, George. You've gone through
          my pockets twenty times. You should
          have got rid of me years ago. I'm no
          good to you, George.

George takes hold of the old man's arms.

                    GEORGE
               (harshly)
          Sit down -- let's go through the
          whole thing from last night.

Hopelessly, Uncle Billy shakes his head.

                    GEORGE (cont'd)
          Just close your eyes -- see a picture --
          can you see a picture of the bills? Were
          they new? Old?

                    UNCLE BILLY
          New, crisp, fresh, smart.

                                        (CONTINUED)

                         GEORGE
          You were alone in the office?

                         UNCLE BILLY
          All alone.

                         GEORGE
          No one cleaning up?

                         UNCLE BILLY
          All alone. I remember putting a rubber
          band around the bills.
               (with a flash of
                memory)
          Yes! Now I remember! I put them
          in the envelope.

                         GEORGE
               (hopefully)
          And put it in your pocket?

                         UNCLE BILLY
               (thinking hard)
          Yes. No. Yes. No. Maybe --
          maybe not.
               (piteously)
          Maybe, Georgie --

                         GEORGE
               (shouts)
          Maybe! I don't want any maybe! We've
          got to find that money, do you hear?
          We've got to find it! Do you know what
          it means if we don't?

                         UNCLE BILLY
          I'm no good --

All this time, George has been holding onto the old
man fiercely, like a drowning man hanging onto a raft.

CLOSE SHOT - the two. Uncle Billy stands before
George like a frisked criminal, all his pockets hanging
out, empty. George's eyes and manner are almost
maniacal.

                         GEORGE
          Where's that money, where's
          that money! Think - think!

Uncle Billy breaks down and sobs.

                                        (CONTINUED)

                              UNCLE BILLY
             I can't think any more, George -
             I can't think any more - it hurts -

                               GEORGE
                        (screaming at him)
             Know what this means, you stupid
             --silly old fool! This means scandal!
             Bankruptcy! Prison! One of us is
             going to jail - and it won't be me!

He turns and CAMERA PANS WITH him as he grabs his
coat and exits, slamming the door behind him.

CLOSE SHOT - Uncle Billy. Anguished he stands a
moment, then sinks into a chair and buries his face
in his hands, weeping, as we

                                              DISSOLVE

INT. GEORGE'S LIVING ROOM - (6:00 PM)

CLOSE SHOT - A piano keyboard. Janie's fingers are
in the shot, as we PULL BACK CAMERA it reveals Janie
(aged eight) practicing a Christmas carol, which she
will pound away on during the balance of the scene.
There is a Christmas tree all decorated near the
fireplace. At a large table Mary is busy putting
cellophane bows and curlicues on gift packages. At
a smaller table Pete (aged nine) is seated with pad
and pencil. He is in the throes of composition. On
the floor is Tommy (aged three) trying to wrap a
Christmas package. We hear the SOUND of a door open
and close. Mary turns and sees George enter room, a
slight powdering of snow on his head and shoulders.
The kids pay no attention, being absorbed in what
they are doing. As Mary comes over to George, his
face suddenly contorts and he sneezes violently.

                               MARY
             Hello, darling.
                        (indicating tree,
                         lights, etc.)
             How do you like it? We've been waiting
             for you to put the star at the top.

George sneezes.

                              FAMILY
             Bless you!

                                              (CONTINUED)

                    MARY
          Did you bring the wreath?

                    GEORGE

          Wreath? What wreath?

                    MARY
          The Merry Christmas wreath for the
          window.

                    GEORGE
          Oh that, yeah. I left it at the
          office.

Mary stares at him aware that something unusual has
happened.

                    MARY
          Is it snowing?

                    GEORGE
          Yeah, just started.

                    MARY
          Where's your hat and coat - and muffler?

                    GEORGE
          Left them at the office too.

                    MARY
          What's the matter?

                    GEORGE
          Nothing's the matter.

                    MARY
          Pete, you put the star up, you're a
          big boy.

                    GEORGE
               (annoyed at
                Janie's playing)
          Must she keep playing that?

                    JANIE
          I have to practice for the party
          tonight, Daddy.

                                        (CONTINUED)

                          PETE
          Mamma says we can stay up 'til
          midnight and sing Christmas carols.

                          TOMMY
          Can you sing, Daddy?

                          MARY
          Better hurry and shave. The
          families will be here soon.

                          GEORGE
          Families! What families. The can't
          come here tonight!

                          MARY
          Come on out in the kitchen while I
          finish dinner.

She leads him out toward kitchen.

CLOSE SHOT - Tommy

                          TOMMY
               (to George)
          Excuse me.

George and Mary pay no attention, but continue toward
kitchen.

                          MARY
          Have a hectic day?

                          GEORGE
               (following her)
          Yeah. Another red-letter day for
          the Bailey's.

                          PETE
               (stopping him)
          Daddy, the Brown's next door have
          a new car - you should see it --

                          GEORGE
               (turning on him
                savagely)
          What's the matter with our car?
          Isn't it good enough for you?

                          PETE
               (frightened at
                his tone)
          Yes, Daddy.

(CONTINUED)

                    TOMMY
          (louder)
     Excuse me!

                    GEORGE
     Excuse you - for what?

                    TOMMY
     I burped!

                    MARY
     You're excused. Now go up and see
     Zuzu.

George ignores him and follows Mary into the kitchen.

                    GEORGE
     What's the matter with Zuzu?

                    MARY
     She's got a cold. Caught it coming
     home from school. They gave her a
     flower for a prize. She didn't want
     to crush the flower so she didn't button
     up her coat....

                    GEORGE
     Sore throat or what is it?

                    MARY
     The doctor says it's nothing serious.

                    GEORGE
     The doctor? Was he here?

                    MARY
     Yes.

                    GEORGE
     Kid running a temperature?

                    MARY
     Just a teensy one - ninety-nine,
     six. She'll be all right.

                    GEORGE
          (with futile rage)
     It's this house! Wonder we don't all
     have pneumonia. This drafty old barn!
     Might as well live in a refrigerator!
     Why did we ever stay in this crummy
     old town?

                                   (CONTINUED)

                              MARY
                    George, what's wrong?

                              GEORGE
                    Everything's wrong! Call this a
                    happy family? And did we have to have
                    all these kids?

                              PETE
                         (coming in)
                    Dad, how do you spell frankincense?

                              GEORGE
                         (shouts)
                    I don't know! Ask your mother.

He starts into the hallway.

                              MARY
                    Where're you going?

                              GEORGE
                    Up to see Zuzu.

We hear his footsteps going up the steps. Mary looks
after him, puzzled and concerned, then comes over
toward Pete.

                              MARY
                    F-R-A-N-K-I-N-C-E-N-S-E.

INT. ZUZU'S ROOM

FULL SHOT. The SOUND OF Janie at the piano can be
heard, the same monotonous rhythm over and over.
Zuzu is sitting up in her bed, the lamp burning beside
her. She is holding her prize flower in a glass.
George tiptoes in. Then, as he sees she's awake, he
comes over, sitting on the edge of her bed.

                              ZUZU
                    Hi, Daddy.

                              GEORGE
                    Well, what happened to you?

                              ZUZU
                    I won a flower.

She starts to get out of bed.

                                        (CONTINUED)

                              GEORGE
          Where do you think you're going?

                              ZUZU
          Want to give my flower a drink.

                              GEORGE
          Here, let me --

She shakes her head and presses the flower to her.
A petal falls off. She picks it up.

                              ZUZU
          Oh look, Daddy, paste it.
                    (on the verge of
                       tears)
          Paste it, Daddy --

                              GEORGE
          Okay, Okay...all right, I'll paste it.

She hands him the fallen petal and the flower. He
turns his back to Zuzu, pretending to be tinkering
with the flower. He sticks the fallen petal in his
watch pocket, re-arranges the flower, and then turns
back to Zuzu.

                              GEORGE (cont'd)
          There it is, good as new.

Zuzu watches him as he puts the glass on the bedside
table.

                              GEORGE
          Now, will you do something for me?

                              ZUZU
          What?

                              GEORGE
          Try to get to sleep.

                              ZUZU
          I'm not sleepy. I want to look at
          my flower.

                              GEORGE
                    (gently)
          If you go to sleep you'll dream about
          it, and it'll be a whole garden.

                              ZUZU
          It will?

                         GEORGE
             Close your eyes.

                         ZUZU
          Aren't you going to kiss me, Daddy?

She closes her eyes and relaxes in the bed. George
pulls the covers over her.

CLOSER ANGLE. George looks long and tenderly at Zuzu.
He bends down and his lips touch a tendril of the
child's hair. Then he gets up and tiptoes out of the
room again. The minute he's gone, Zuzu opens her
eyes, sits up, reaches toward the glass with the
flower and holds it close to her breast.

INT. HALLWAY

FULL SHOT - George is coming down the stairs, his
face set and scowling.

                         MARY
                  (on phone)
             Hello...Yes, this is Mrs. Bailey --

George looks over toward:

CLOSE SHOT - Pete, writing his Christmas play.
CAMERA PANS OVER TO Janie. With grim determination,
she keeps pounding out her piece.

CLOSE SHOT - George. He looks again at the drawing
of the horse with the three eyes made by Zuzu. Into
shot, we hear Mary's voice:

                       MARY'S VOICE
             Thank you, Mrs. Welch, I'm sure
             she'll be all right --

At the mention of Mrs. Welch, George goes tense. He
turns and exits into hallway.

INT. HALLWAY

CLOSE SHOT at phone as George enters shot; Mary is
saying:

                              MARY
                    The doctor says she ought to be out
                    of bed in time to have her Christmas
                    dinner --

                              GEORGE
                    Is that Zuzu's teacher?

                              MARY
                         (hand over mouthpiece)
                    Yes.

                              GEORGE
                    Let me speak to her.

Mary watches him, startled. His expression is irate,
his voice harsh and truculent.

                              GEORGE
                         (on phone)
                    Hello, Mrs. Welch? This is George
                    Bailey. I'm Zuzu's father. What kind
                    of a teacher are you? What do you mean
                    by sending her home like that, half
                    naked? Do you realize she might end
                    up with pneumonia on account of you?

                              MARY
                         (shocked)
                    George!

She puts a restraining hand on his arm. He shakes it
off. She cannot know that George's tirade against
Mrs. Welch is really a tirade against the world, against
life, against God. Over the phone we hear Mrs. Welch's
voice sputtering with protest.

                              GEORGE
                    Is that the kind of thing we pay taxes
                    for -- to have teachers like you? Silly,
                    stupid, careless people who send kids
                    home without their coats! Maybe my children
                    aren't the best-dressed kids -- maybe they
                    don't have decent clothes -- is that any
                    reason --

Mary is tugging at his arm, but he shakes her off again.
We hear Mrs. Welch's voice squawking on the phone in
indignant comeback, the general import of which nobody
has ever talked to her like that before and she doesn't
have to stand for it and she won't.

                                            (CONTINUED)

                          MARY
          Mrs. Welch -- please -- I want to
          apologize -- Hello -- hello --
                (to George
                  wrathfully)
          She's hung up.

                          GEORGE
          I'll hang her up!

But the earpiece is suddenly alive with a powerful
male voice, calling:

                     VOICE ON PHONE
          How, who do you think you are!

George hears this and grabs the receiver from Mary.

                          GEORGE
                (into phone)
          Who is this? Mr.Welch? Well, this is
          Mrs. Bailey's husband...okay...give
          me a chance to tell you what I think
          of your wife.
                (to Mary)
          Will you go away and let me handle
          this?
                (into phone)
          You will, huh? Okay...any time you
          think you're man enough.
                (before he can think
                  up an insult to top
                  Welch's, we hear a
                  click on the telephone.
                  George turns to Mary)
          He hung up.

George starts into living room.

                          PETE
          Dad - how do you spell "hallelujah?"

                          GEORGE
          I don't know. What do you think I am -
          a dictionary? You, Janie - don't
          you know that piece yet? Over and
          over! Stop it!

The piano music comes to an abrupt stop. George's face
is flushed and wet. His attention goes to one of his
modern building models. He gives it a vicious kick
and smashes it to pieces.

                                        (CONTINUED)

                              GEORGE (cont'd)
            I went off the handle there.

He looks around and sees Mary, Peter and Janie staring
at him as if he were some unknown wild animal.

                              GEORGE (cont'd)
            Sorry, Mary.

Mary is too hurt to answer.

                              GEORGE (cont'd)
            Sorry, Janie -- I didn't mean --
            go ahead, you can practice.

Janie sits staring at him.

                              GEORGE (cont'd)
            Pete, I owe you an apology, too.
            Now, what was it you wanted?

Pete stares at him, trying to hold back the tears.

                              PETE
            Nothing, Daddy.

                              GEORGE
                 (harshly)
            What are you crying about?
                 (to Janie)
            And you, Janie, why don't you play?

Janie breaks into sobs.

                              JANIE
                 (still looking
                  at him)
            Oh, Daddy --

                              MARY
                 (in an outburst)
            George! Must you torture the
            children, too? Why don't you --

The sight of his children suffering is too much for
George. Almost breaking he goes over to Janie and
holds her.

                              GEORGE
            Oh, Janie, I'm sorry.

Then he quickly goes out the front door.

                                          (CONTINUED)

EXT. PORCH

Snow falling. George leans up against a pillar,
deeply hurt and miserable at the suffering he has
caused. Mary comes out quietly and takes his arm.
She knows there is something terribly wrong. The
following scene is played quietly and tenderly.

                    MARY
          I'm sorry dear.

                    GEORGE
               (embracing her)
          Mary Hatch - please believe me.
          Mary Hatch, I love you, very
          very much.

He kisses her tenderly and walks down steps.

CLOSE SHOT- Mary, dismayed and bewildered. She
stands rooted to the spot for a moment, then, getting
an idea she turns and hurries inside.

INT. LIVING ROOM. Mary comes in and goes to telephone.
Pete, Janie and Tommy run to her, still tear-stained.

                    PETER
          Is Daddy in trouble?

                    MARY
          Yes, Peter.

                    JANIE
          Shall I pray for him?

                    MARY
          Yes, Janie - pray very hard.

                    TOMMY
          Me too?

                    MARY
          You too, Tommy,

She starts dialing a number.

                                   DISSOLVE OUT

DISSOLVE IN

INT. POTTER'S OFFICE - NIGHT 8:00 P.M.

MED. SHOT. Potter is seated at his desk, his head
bent, engrossed with some papers as the door opens
and George enters. Potter addresses him without
looking up.

> POTTER
> Yes. What can I do for you, George?

> GEORGE
> Well, some years ago, Mr. Potter, you
> may remember, you were kind enough
> to make me a sort of a proposition
> about coming in with you -

> POTTER
> Yes. I shall never forget it. I
> offered you a three-year contract at
> twenty thousand a year. You called
> me a scurvy little spider.

> GEORGE
> I was wrong, Mr. Potter. I was a
> fool, and I was wondering if the
> offer still stands.

Potter concentrates on his papers.

> POTTER
> I knew that some day you'd come
> crawling in here on your hands and
> knees.

> GEORGE
> If you want me to get on my knees,
> I'll be glad to do it. I'm in
> trouble, Mr. Potter. I need help.

Potter does not look up.

> GEORGE (cont'd)
> Through an accident my company is
> short in its accounts. The bank
> examiner came today. I've got to raise
> eight thousand dollars immediately.

> POTTER
> Oh, that's the reason the reporters are
> looking for you.

> GEORGE
> The reporters?

(CONTINUED)

                         POTTER
        Yes, they called from your Building
        and Loan. The man from the D.A.'s
        office is there, too.

                         GEORGE
        Please help me, Mr. Potter. I'd be
        glad to pay you a bonus for the loan -
        any interest -- if you still want the
        Building and Loan - why - I --

                         POTTER
        It couldn't be that there was a
        slight discrepancy in the books, could
        it, George?

                         GEORGE
        No sir, nothing wrong with the books -
        I've misplaced eight thousand dollars -
        can't find it anywhere.

                         POTTER
             (looking up)
        You misplaced it? Well, why didn't
        you report it to the police?

                         GEORGE
        I didn't want any publicity. It
        would spoil Harry's homecoming.

                         POTTER
        They'll believe that one.
             (slyly)
        What've you been doing, George, playing
        the market with the company's money?

                         GEORGE
        No sir, no sir.

                         POTTER
        Then what is it - a woman? It's all
        over town you've been giving money to
        Violet Bick?
             (shrugs)
        Anyhow, why come to me? Why don't you
        ask Sam Wainwright?

                         GEORGE
        I can't get him. He's in Europe.

                         POTTER
        What about all your other friends?

                                          (CONTINUED)

                         GEORGE
They haven't got that kind of
money, Mr. Potter. You're the
only man in town that can help me.

                         POTTER
I see, I see -- I've suddenly become
important. What sort of security
would I have? Have you any stock?

                         GEORGE
No, sir.

                         POTTER
Bonds? Real estate? Collateral of
any kind?

                         GEORGE
          (pulls out policy)
I have some life insurance -- a
fifteen thousand dollar policy.

                         POTTER
How much is your equity in it?

                         GEORGE
About five hundred dollars.

                         POTTER
Five hundred! And you ask me to lend
you eight thousand. Do you call that
good business?
          (contemptuously)
Look at you - couldn't even get in the
Army! You used to be so cocky! You
were gonna go out and conquer the world.
You once called me a warped frustrated
old man. Well, what are you but a warped
frustrated young man. A miserable little
clerk crawling on your hands and knees
begging for help. Married ten years,
four children and you still live in a
house the bats moved out of twenty years
ago. No securities - no stocks - no
bonds - nothing but a measly five
hundred dollar equity in a life insurance
policy. You're worth more dead than alive.
Why don't you go to the riff-raff you love
so much and ask them for eight thousand.
Know why? Because they'd run you out of
town on a rail. But I'll tell you what
I'm going to do as a stockholder in the
Building & Loan for you, young man: as
long as the State Examiner's here, I'm
going to swear out a warrant for your
arrest! Misappropriation of funds -
manipulation - malfeasance -

                                  (CONTINUED)

George turns and starts out as Potter picks up the
telephone and dials.

                    POTTER (cont'd)
          Go on - Go on -- That's all right!
          Go! You can't hide in a little town
          like this!

George is out of the door by now. CAMERA MOVES
CLOSER to Potter on telephone.

                    POTTER
          Bill, this is Potter. Quite well
          thank you. Merry Xmas to you. Say
          Bill, there's a little matter you can
          straighten out for me if you will.
          It's about Bailey - George Bailey.

EXT. BEDFORD FALLS STREET - NIGHT - SNOWING

George runs from bank to his car. He has just been
turned down by Potter. George gets in his car. As
he does so, Bert, the cop, drives up alongside in
his State Police car. He stops opposite George.

                    BERT
          Hi, George. Glad I saw you. I'm on
          duty tonight -- save me a trip to
          your house.
               (passes over some
                Xmas packages)
          Here're some little things for the
          kids -- one here especially for Zuzu.
          She's my gal.

                    GEORGE
               (trying to hide
                his emotional
                disturbance)
          Thanks, Bert.

                    BERT
          I'm leading the parade tomorrow for
          Harry. Boy, I can't wait to see the guy.
          Guess the Bailey clan'll be hard to get
          along with from now on, eh?
               (honks behind
                him. Cars are
                lining up)
          Better beat it before I lead
          another parade. Merry Christmas,
          George. See you on the front page.

George drives off furiously.

                                        (CONTINUED)

EXT. MAIN STREET - NIGHT (8:30 PM)

CLOSE MOVING SHOT - Mrs. Bailey. Her arms laden with
Christmas packages and her head bowed against the storm,
she's on her way down the street when her attention
is attracted by:

EXT. STREET - NIGHT

MED. SHOT. George is driving by in his car. He does
not see his mother and he does not hear her call his
name, but continues right on past her. She turns and
takes a few steps after the car. He voice can be
faintly heard, calling after him.

                          MRS. BAILEY'S VOICE
          George!....George!....

                                    DISSOLVE

INT. MARTINI'S PLACE - NIGHT (9:30 PM)

CLOSE SHOT - bar mirror - MUSIC and SOUND effects.
Framed by wine bottles and Christmas decorations, we
see George's reflection in the mirror. CAMERA PULLS
BACK to take in George standing at the bar. And now,
in the mirror, with a WIDENED FOCUS OF CAMERA, we get
a glimpse of the place, which is an Italian restaurant
with bar. The bottles sparkle, there are Christmas
greens and holly decorating the place. It has a warm,
welcoming spirit, like Martini himself, who is behind
the bar assisting the bartender with the Christmas
trade. The booths and the checkered cloth-covered
tables are full. There is an air of festivity and
friendliness, and more like a party than a public
drinking place.

CLOSE SHOT - REVERSE ANGLE - George. He has had a
great deal to drink, far more than he's accustomed
to. CAMERA has to get VERY CLOSE TO him before we
hear what he is mumbling.

                          GEORGE
                    (mumbling)
          Dear Father in Heaven, I'm not a
          praying man, but if You're up there,
          God, and You can hear me - show me
          the way. I'm at the end of my rope.
          Show me the way - show me the way....

                                    (CONTINUED)

We can barely make out the actual wording of George's
prayer. We get just enough of it to identify the
prayer we heard at the beginning of the picture.
During this CAMERA ANGLE WIDENS TO take in a man
standing at the bar near George. He's a burly
individual, drinking a glass of beer between pulls
on a pipe. In the mirror we see a customer go up
and deposit a coin in the juke box and the instant
it blares out its cheap song, the other SOUNDS are
BLOTTED OUT, and George's head comes up. As he
looks up, Nick, the bartender comes into shot.

                    NICK
               (friendly)
          Feel all right? Anything I can do
          for you, George? Want someone to
          take you home?

Nick beckons to Martini, who comes up to George.

                    MARTINI
          Why you drink so much, my friend?
          Please go home, Mr. Bailey. This is
          Christmas Eve.

The ugly man next to George, who has been listening,
reacts sharply to the name, "Bailey."

                    BURLEY MAN
               (to George)
          Bailey? Which Bailey?

                    MARTIN
          Mr. George Bailey.

Without warning the Ugly Man throws a vicious punch
at George, who goes down and out. Martini and
several others rush to pick him up. Nick grabs
bottle and stands poised behind bar.

                    BURLEY MAN
          And the next time you talk to my
          wife like that you'll get worse!
          She cried for an hour. It isn't
          enough she has to slave to teach
          your stupid kids to read and write,
          but you go and bawl her out --

                    MARTINI
               (furious)
          You get out of here, Mr. Welch.

                                   (CONTINUED)

Man reaches in pocket for money.

                    MARTINI (cont'd)
          Never mind the money -- you get out
          quick. You hit my friend -- get out.

The Ugly Man walks out. George comes to. He is helped
to his feet by a waiter and Martini.

                    NICK
          You all right, George?

                    GEORGE
               (stunned)
          Where's he? Who was 'at?

                    MARTINI
          Don't worry. He gone. Name is Welch.
          He don't come to my place no more.

                    GEORGE
          Oh - Welch. Well, he was right.
          That's what I get for praying.

George gulps down the drink he had left.

                    MARTINI
          Last time he come in here.
          Hear that, Nick?

                    NICK
          Yes -- you bet.

                    GEORGE
          Policy? Where's my insurance policy?
               (he finds it in pocket)
          Sorry.
               (he starts for door)

Martini follows him solicitously.

                    MARTINI
          Mr. Bailey, don't go out that way.
          Stay here. Sit down and rest.

                    GEORGE
               (going on)
          I'm all right.

                                        (CONTINUED)

                    MARTINI
        You don't feel so good. Stay here.

                    GEORGE
                (roughly shaking
                 him off)
        I'm all right.

CAMERA FOLLOWS George as he goes to door, wobbly,
angry, desperate. Martini looks after him unhappily.

EXT. MARTINI'S RESTAURANT - NIGHT

FULL SHOT. An electric sign flashes off and on,
advertising "MARTINI'S RESTAURANT AND BAR - ITALIAN
DISHES" etc. George comes out and climbs unsteadily
into his car. In his stunned condition, he forgets
to turn on the headlights of his car. As he starts
the car down the street, a man's voice calls to him.

                    MAN'S VOICE
        Lights! Lights! Put your lights on,
        you dumb egg!

But George's car goes on down the street with the
lights still off.

                                        DISSOLVE

EXT. STREET - NIGHT

FULL SHOT - the car comes along the empty street, and
suddenly swerves, crashing into a tree near the
sidewalk on the lawn of a modest home. As George
starts slowly to get out, the owner of the house
rushes out and comes running to him.

                    OWNER
        Hey, what do you think you're doing?

CLOSER ANGLE - George stands unsteadily near the car,
shaken by the accident. The front lights are broken
and the fender is ripped. George stands dully looking
at the damage. The owner comes up, looking at his
tree. He leans over to examine the damages.

                    OWNER
                (shrill
                 indignation)
        Now, see what you've done!
                (indicates great gash
                 in tree)
        My great-grandfather planted that tree.

                                        (CONTINUED)

                         GEORGE
                    (morosely)
          Is your great-grandfather still alive?

                         OWNER
          No.

                         GEORGE
          Then what does he care?

He starts to walk away, leaving the car and going
toward the river. The owner, absorbed in the
examination of the tree's injury, turns and sees
that George is gone.

                         OWNER
          Hey, you! <u>You</u>!

CLOSE MOVING SHOT - George. He walks toward the
river as if in a trance. The owner's voice is heard,
diminuendo.

                         OWNER'S VOICE
          Come back here you drunken fool!
          Take this car out of here! Take
          it out before I call the police!

George walks on, not heeding anything, his eyes on
the river ahead. There is the SOUND of a truck coming
along the road. The horn SOUNDS, and then SOUNDS
again, imperatively. George goes on, not hearing it.

WIDER ANGLE - MOVING SHOT. The truck swerves in a
wide angle to pass George. The driver shouts at
George, but the wind carries his words away. The
truck turns to go over the bridge. George takes a
narrow catwalk at the railing.

MED. SHOT - At center of bridge. George comes up to
the center and stops, looking down at the dark moving
water.

CLOSEUP - Toll house. Toll keeper is eyeing George
suspiciously.

                                        (CONTINUED)

CLOSE SHOT - Geroge. He stares down at the water,
desperate, trying to make up his mind to act. He
takes Zuzu's flower petals from his pocket, looks
at them, then carefully puts them back. He leans
over looking at the water, fascinated. The moaning
of the wind takes on a peculiar, eerie sound, as
though done by a great many harps. Slowly, George
starts to remove his coat. ALL SOUND DIES DOWN.
There is now absolute silence. This is broken by
the SOUND of a loud splash in the water. George
looks down into the water, reacting to:

EXT. RIVER

FULL SHOT - George's point of view. From the water,
where the splash has occurred, a head emerges and
a voice calls out:

                         VOICE
        Help! -- Help!

FULL SHOT - River. George climbs over the rail and
plunges in after the man.

CLOSER ANGLE. George comes up, sees the man flailing
about in the water and CAMERA PANS WITH him as he
swims toward the man. A spotlight lights up a
circle on the water.

CLOSE SHOT - bridge rail. Tollkeeper is anxiously
peering into the water trying to find the man with
his flashlight.

CLOSE SHOT. The man in the water is Clarence. George
reaches him and grabs hold of him. Clarence struggles
excitedly. George, a veteran Boy Scout, knows just
what to do. He socks Clarence right on the button.
Then as he starts swimming with him,

                                        WIPE

INT. BRIDGE TOLL HOUSE - NIGHT

MED. SHOT - George, Clarence and tollkeeper. George
is seated before a wood stove near which his clothes
are draped. He is naked, being partially hidden by
the hanging clothes. He stares at the fire, cold,

                                        (CONTINUED)

gloomy and drunk, ignoring Clarence and the tollkeeper,
preoccupied by his near suicide and his unsolved
problems. Clarence is standing alongside, naked.
He is testing his undershirt to see if it's dry. This
is a ludicrous Seventeenth Century garment which
looks like a baby's night shirt - with embroidered
cuffs and collar, and gathered at the neck with a
drawstring. It falls halfway to Clarence's knees.

The tollkeeper, a droopy-mustached old codger, smoking
a vicious-looking pipe, is seated against the wall
eyeing them suspiciously. Throughout the scene he
attempts to spit, but each time is stopped by some
amazing thing Clarence does or says.

Clarence, feeling his undershirt is dry enough, puts
it on over his head. He becomes aware that his
garment is amazing the tollkeeper.

                    CLARENCE
               (apologizing)
          I didn't have time to get some
          stylish underwear --
               (nostalgically)
          Wife gave me this on my last
          birthday. I passed away in it.

The tollkeeper, about to spit, is stopped in the
middle of it by this remark. Clarence, secretly
trying to get George's attention, now picks up Tom
Sawyer book which has been drying out.

                    CLARENCE
          Tom Sawyer's drying out, too.
          You should read the new book.
          Mark Twain's writing now --

                    TOLLKEEPER
          How'd you happen to fall in?

                    CLARENCE
          Huh? Oh, I didn't fall in. I
          jumped in to save George.

                    GEORGE
               (coming to life)
          To save me!

                    CLARENCE
               (smiling at him)
          Well, I did, didn't I? You didn't
          go through with it, did you?

                                        (CONTINUED)

                         GEORGE
          With what?

                         CLARENCE
          Suicide.

George and Tollkeeper react to this.

                         TOLLKEEPER
          It's against the law to commit
          suicide around here.

                         CLARENCE
          It's against the law where I come
          from, too.

                         TOLLKEEPER
               (in a haze)
          Where do you come from?

                         CLARENCE
               (simply)
          Heaven.

Tollkeeper is interrupted in another attempt to spit.
George dismisses the answer hazily, and goes back to
brooding.

                         CLARENCE (cont'd)
          Yes, yes, I had to act quickly.
          That's why I jumped in. I knew if
          I were drowning you'd try to save me.
          And you see, you did -- that's how
          I saved you.

Tollkeeper becomes increasingly nervous. George
casually looks at the strange smiling little man a
second time.

                         GEORGE
               (off hand)
          Yeah. Very funny.

                         CLARENCE
          Your lip's bleeding, George.

George's hand goes to his mouth.

                         GEORGE
          Got a bust in the jaw in answer to --

                              (CONTINUED)

                         CLARENCE
          Oh, no, George, I'm the answer to
          your prayers. That's why I was sent
          down here.

                         GEORGE
                 (casually interested)
          How do you know my name?

                         CLARENCE
          Oh, I know all about you. I've watched
          you grow up from a little boy.

                         GEORGE
          What are you, a mind reader?

                         CLARENCE
          Oh, no.

                         GEORGE
                 (laughing)
          Well, then, who are you?

                         CLARENCE
          I'm Clarence Odbody, AS 2.

                         GEORGE
          AS 2?

                         CLARENCE
          Angel Second Class.

The tollkeeper's chair slips out from under him. He
has been leaning against the wall on it, tipped back
on two legs. Tollkeeper rises and makes his way out
warily toward the door. From his expression he looks
like he'll call the nearest cop.

                         TOLLKEEPER
          Gotta go out now. Bridge opening.

                         CLARENCE
          Cheerio, my good man.

Tollkeeper back out. George holds his head.

                         GEORGE
          Brother, I wonder what Martini puts
          in that liquor.
                 (to Clarence)
          What was that you were saying?
          Why'd you want to save me?

                                          (CONTINUED)

                          CLARENCE
That's why I was sent down here.
I'm your Guardian Angel.

                          GEORGE
Wouldn't be a bit surprised.

                          CLARENCE
Ridiculous of you to think of
killing yourself for money. Eight
thousand dollars --

                          GEORGE
That's another thing -- huh? How'd
you know that?

                          CLARENCE
I told you, I'm your Guardian Angel.
I know everything about you.

                          GEORGE
Well you look like the kind of an angel
I'd get. Fallen agnel, huh? What
became of your wings?

                          CLARENCE
I haven't won my wings yet. That's
why I'm an Angel Second Class.

                          GEORGE
Well, I don't know as I'd like to
be seen around with an angel who hasn't
got wings.

                          CLARENCE
Oh, I got to earn them - and you'll
help me, won't you?

                          GEORGE
Sure. Sure. How?

                          CLARENCE
By letting me help you.

                          GEORGE
Only one way you can help me.

                          CLARENCE
How?

                                    (CONTINUED)

                    GEORGE
Have you got eight thousand
dollars?

                    CLARENCE
No, no, no, George. We have no use
for money in heaven.

                    GEORGE
It's pretty handy down here. I found
it out too late. That's why I'm
worth more dead than alive.

                    CLARENCE
Now look, you mustn't talk that way,
I won't get my wings with that attitude.
You just don't know all that you've done.
If it hand't been for you --

                    GEORGE
If it hadn't been for me, everybody
would have been better off. My wife,
kids, friends. Look will you leave me
alone?

                    CLARENCE
I can't leave you alone - I've got
a job to do.

                    GEORGE
Aw, shut up.

                    CLARENCE
So you still think killing yourself
would make everyone feel happier?

                    GEORGE
Huh? Guess you're right. I guess maybe
it would have been better if I'd never
been born at all.

                    CLARENCE
What'd you say?

                    GEORGE
I say I wish I'd never been born.

                    CLARENCE
You mustn't say things like that.
Wait a minute - that's an idea.
     (looks to heaven)
What do you think?

                         CLARENCE (cont'd)
               (to himself)
          That'll do it!
               (to George)
          All right, you've got your wish.
          You've never been born.

The snow stops - wind begins to blow - door bangs
open. Clarence runs and closes it.

                         CLARENCE (cont'd)
               (to heaven)
          Well, you don't have to make all
          that fuss about it.

                         GEORGE
          What?

                         CLARENCE
          You've never been born. You don't
          exist. You haven't a care in the
          world -- no worries -- no obligations --
          no eight thousand dollars to get -- no
          Potter looking for you with the Sheriff --

As Clarence speaks, George cocks his head curiously,
favoring his deaf ear, more interested in his hearing
than in what Clarence has said.

                         GEORGE
               (favoring his
                deaf ear)
          Hey, say something in this ear.

                         CLARENCE
          Sure you can hear out of it.

                         GEORGE
          That's the doggonedest thing --
          First time I've heard out of that
          ear since I was a kid! Maybe it
          was the jump in the cold water.

                         CLARENCE
          Your lip's stopped bleeding, too.

George puts his hand up to his lip. No cut, no
swelling. His bewilderment is comical.

                          GEORGE
     What's happened? I must be -- it's
     stopped snowing -
               (shrugs and gives up)
     I'm all mixed up. Haven't the nerve
     to jump in that river again - I need
     a couple of stiff drinks that's for
     sure. How about you angel, want a
     drink?

                          CLARENCE
               (interrupting)
     Our clothes are dry.

George feels the clothes. They are perfectly dry.

                          GEORGE
     So they are. Stove's hotter'n
     I thought. Come on, angel.

They start to dress.

                          GEORGE (cont'd)
     We'll stroll over to my car and --
     oh, I'm sorry. I'll stroll and you
     fly.

                          CLARENCE
     But I can't fly -- I haven't got my
     wings.

                          GEORGE
               (repeating last
                phrase with him)
     You haven't got your wings.
     Okay, a couple of drinks and we'll
     both fly.

                                        DISSOLVE

EXT. STREET - NIGHT

MED. SHOT. This is the same empty street where
George's car swerved into the tree near the sidewalk.
George and Clarence come into shot and up to tree
where George has left his car buckled against the
tree.

CLOSER ANGLE. George looks around, bewildered.

                                        (CONTINUED)

                         CLARENCE
          What's the matter?

                         GEORGE
          This is where I left my car and it
          isn't here.

                         CLARENCE
          You have no car.

                         GEORGE
          Well, I had a car and it was right
          here. Someone must've taken it away.

CLOSE SHOT at curb. A car drives up, and the owner
of the house gets out. He has some Christmas
packages.

                         THE OWNER
               (politely)
          Good evening.

                         GEORGE
          Where's my car?

                         THE OWNER
          Beg pardon?

                         GEORGE
          I'm the fellow who owns the car that
          ran into your tree?

                         THE OWNER
          What tree?

                         GEORGE
               (indicates o.s.)
          That one.

The owner looks sharply at George and starts out of
shot.

CLOSE SHOT at tree. Clarence stands waiting as George
and the owner come into shot. The owner takes out a
cigarette lighter, ignites it and begins to examine
the tree. He finds the trunk unscarred and looks up,
relieved.

                                   (CONTINUED)

                          THE OWNER
                    (quizzically)
          I guess you must've meant two other
          trees.

George takes the cigarette lighter from his hand and
feverishly begins to look all around the trunk of the
tree. The bark is untouched. He straightens up,
utterly bewildered.

                          THE OWNER (cont'd)
          You had me worried. I have a great
          sentiment for that tree. My great-
          grandfather planted it. That's one
          of the oldest trees in Pottersville.

                          GEORGE
                    (blankly)
          Pottersville? You mean Bedford Falls?

                          THE OWNER
          I mean Pottersville.
                    (sharply)
          Don't you think I know where I live.
          What's the matter with you?

Scowling, he exits back to his house. George stares
after him and then turns to Clarence.

                          GEORGE
          I'm either off my nut -- or that
          guy is -- or you are.

He runs his hands over the bark of the tree to make
sure.

                          GEORGE (cont'd)
          It isn't him.

                          CLARENCE
                    (smugly)
          It isn't me.

George puts his hands to his head and tries to get his
dizzy mind to focus again.

                          GEORGE
          Maybe I left it at Martini's.
                    (increasingly edgy)
          All right, come on, Gabriel.

                          CLARENCE
          Clarence.

As they start away -

                                        DISSOLVE
                                    (CONTINUED)

INT. MARTINI'S PLACE

The cheerful Italian feeling is gone. It is now more
of a hard-drinking joint, a honky-tonk. Same bar,
tables have no covers. People are lower down and
tougher. Nick the Bartender, now a tough hard-boiled
hombre, is behind the bar. George and Clarence come
in. George does not notice any difference, but
Clarence is all eyes and beaming. They go up to bar.
Nick fixes them with a look as they talk.

                    GEORGE
          Good friend of mine, Martini. Should
          apologize to him for the way I left
          this place half hour ago. Hi'ya Nick,
          where's Martini?

                    NICK
          You wanna Martini?

                    GEORGE
          No jokes now, Nick. Your boss?
          Where's your boss?

                    NICK
          Look, fella - I'm the boss. Wanna
          drink or don't yuh?

                    GEORGE
          Oh sure, Nick - double bourbon, quick.

                    NICK
               (to Clarence)
          What's yours?

                    CLARENCE
          I was just thinking.
               (face puckers up with
                delicious anticipation)
          - It's been so long -- yes -
          yes - tch! Tch!

                    NICK
               (pointedly)
          I'm standing here, mister, waiting
          for you to make up your mind.

                    CLARENCE
               (amiably)
          That's a good lad.

                                      (CONTINUED)

Nick blanches with rage. George seems to enjoy it
and winks knowingly at Nick.

                    CLARENCE (cont'd)
          I was thinking of a flaming rum
          punch. But it's not cold enough for
          that. Not <u>nearly</u> cold enough.
                    (eyes light up
                     with decision)
          I have it - mulled wine; heavy on the
          cinnamon, light on the cloves. Off
          with you, lad, and be lively!

Nick leans forward and addresses Clarence with a
quiet, acid passion.

                    NICK
          Look mister - we serve hard drinks
          for men who want to get drunk fast.
          And we don't want any characters
          around here trying to give the joint
          atmosphere. Is that clear? Or
          should I reach out with my left and
          slip you a convincer?

                    CLARENCE
          What's he talking about?

                    GEORGE
                    (hastily)
          He'll take same as mine.

                    NICK
          Okay! What I hate is every little
          rabbit-faced lush saving up his jokes
          for the nearest bartender.
                    (muttering as he
                     starts off for the drinks)
          His wife won't listen to 'im.
          His kids won't listen to 'im.
          What makes him think <u>I</u> gotta?

                    GEORGE
                    (puzzled)
          I've never seen Nick act like that
          before.

                    CLARENCE
          You'll see a lot of strange things
          from now on.

                              (CONTINUED)

                         GEORGE
                    (moodily)
          Yeah, from a jail window. Look here,
          little fella -- you worry me. Got
          a place to sleep?

                         CLARENCE

          No.

                         GEORGE

          Got any money?

                         CLARENCE

          No.

Nick comes in with drinks and hears this last remark.
He looks from one to the other from no on.

                         GEORGE
          You're worse off than -- No
          wonder you jumped in the river.

                         CLARENCE
                    (heatedly)
          I jumped in to save you so I
          can get my wings.

Nick stops pouring, bottle poised in his hand. A
cash register bell rings. It attracts Clarence's
attention.

                         CLARENCE (cont'd)
          Somebody just made it.

                         GEORGE

          Made what?

                         CLARENCE
          Whenever you hear a bell ring it
          means some angel's got his wings.

                         GEORGE
          If I were you Clarence, I wouldn't
          say anything in here about being an
          angel.

                         CLARENCE
          Don't they believe in angels?

                         GEORGE
          Yes, but -- you know -

                                        (CONTINUED)

                              CLARENCE
              Then why should they be surprised
              when they see one?

                              GEORGE
              He never grew up. By the way, how
              old are you?

                              CLARENCE
              Two hundred and ninety-three --
                   (thinks)
              - next May!

Nick slams the bottle down on the counter.

                              NICK
              That does it! All right, you two
              pixies - get out! Through that door or
              you go through the window.

                              GEORGE
              What's wrong, Nick?

                              NICK
              And where do you get off calling
              me Nick?

                              GEORGE
              That's your name.

                              NICK
              What's that got to do with it? I
              don't know you from Adam's off ox -
                   (sees somebody
                    come in)
              Hey, you! Rummy!

CLOSEUP - a small, wreck of a man, with weak,
watery eyes. Obviously a broken- down panhandler,
his hat in his hand.

                              NICK

              Come here!

CLOSEUP - George. He can hardly believe his eyes.
It is Gower, the druggist.

                              NICK
                   (to Gower)
              How many times have I told you never
              to come in here panhandling?
                   (picks up soda bottle and
                    squirts Gower full in
                    the face.)
              Go around the back. They'll give
              you something to eat.

Gower smiles weakly, and nods as he turns toward
rear.

                    GEORGE
          Mr. Gower!

Gower turns, stares, blinks with his bleary eyes,
then starts out again. George runs over to him.

                    GEORGE (cont'd)
          Mr. Gower! Don't you know me?

Gower shakes his head blankly.

                    GOWER
               (blankly)
          No.

He turns and shuffles off toward the rear. George
strides back to Nick.

                    NICK
          Throw 'em out.

                    GEORGE
               (excited)
          Nick, Nick! Isn't that Mr. Gower,
          the druggist?

                    NICK
          That's one more reason for me not
          liking you -
               (starts around end
                of bar)
          That rum head spent twenty years in
          jail for poisoning a kid. If you know
          him, you must be a jail bird yourself.
               (to waiters)
          Show these gentlemen to the door.

Two waiters grab George and Clarence; give them the
heave-ho toward the door. Nick rings up cash register.

                    NICK (cont'd)
          Hey! I'm giving out wings!
               (laughs and rings
                up cash register)

EXT. MARTINI'S PLACE - NIGHT

                                        (CONTINUED)

George and Clarence come flying through the door and
land in the snow. George has a strange, puzzled look
on his face. The remain for a moment as they landed,
looking at each other.

> CLARENCE
> You see, George, you weren't there
> to stop Gower from putting that
> poison ---

> GEORGE
> What do you mean I wasn't there?
> I remember distinctly -
>> (his eye catches the
>> neon sign over door)

CLOSEUP - sign over door. It now blinks "NICK'S PLACE"
instead of "MARTINI'S."

MED. SHOT. George rises and stares at sign.

> GEORGE
>> (exasperated)
> What the - what's going on around
> here? This should be Martini's place.

He points to the sign and looks at Clarence. Clarence
sort of hangs his head. George fixes him with a very
interested look.

> GEORGE
>> (seriously)
> Look, little man - who are you?

> CLARENCE
> I told you, George - I'm your
> guardian angel.

George, still looking intently at him, goes up to him
and feels his arm. It's flesh.

> GEORGE
> You said all that before. What else
> are you? A hypnotist?

> CLARENCE
> No, of course not.

> GEORGE
> Then what are all these strange things
> I'm seeing?

(CONTINUED)

               CLARENCE
Don't you understand - it's because
you weren't born.

               GEORGE
If I wasn't born, then who am I?

               CLARENCE
You're nobody. You have no identity.

George feels for his wallet.

               GEORGE
What do you mean, no identity.
I'm George Bailey.

               CLARENCE
There is no George Bailey. You have
no papers, no cards, no driver's
license, no 4-F card, no insurance
policy.
        (he says these things
          as George feels for them)
They're not there, either.

               GEORGE

What?

               CLARENCE

Zuzu's petals.

George quickly feels for them in his vest pocket.
They are not there.

               CLARENCE (cont'd)
You've been given a great gift, George -
a chance to see what the world would be
like without you.

               GEORGE
      (groping for
      understanding)
Zuzu's sick - got a temperature -
and I've got to put the star on the
tree -- it's a funny dream I'm having
here -- if you don't mind, mister,
think I'll go home for a minute.

He sort of waves to Clarence and turns.

               (CONTINUED)

                         CLARENCE
        Home?   What home?

                         GEORGE
              (violently)
        Stop it!   Stop it!   You hear -
        you're crazy!   That's what I think,
        and you're driving me crazy, too!
        You've got me seeing things. I'm
        going home - to my wife and kids, and
        I'm going alone.

George strides off hurriedly. Clarence remains behind
looking after him, then slowly starts walking in
his direction. Clarence looks up to heaven.

                         CLARENCE
        How'm I doing, Joseph? Thanks. I
        didn't have a drink.

EXT. BEDFORD FALLS - MAIN STREET - NIGHT

In general the street appears the same, but fewer
people are around. It is still Christmas Eve, but
there doesn't seem to be as many shoppers. Only a
few stores are open and these seem to be mostly
poolrooms, liquor stores and little joint-like
cafes.

George hurries along, impelled by a strange fear.

                         GEORGE
              (to himself)
        They can't arrest me tonight.
        I better take that wreath home to Mary.

He stops short as he sees:

EXT. POTTER'S BANK - NIGHT

MED. SHOT. It is dark. He sees now it is called:

        "POTTERSVILLE FIRST NATIONAL BANK"

He looks up and down the street and sees the name
"Pottersville" on other business fronts. He walks
on faster. Arrives in front of Building and Loan.

EXT. MAIN STREET - NIGHT - CLOSE (MOVING) SHOT - GEORGE

                                      (CONTINUED)

Walking along in a daze, he passes the Building where
formerly had been the Building & Loan Association
offices. He stops, a shocked look in his eyes as he
sees:

FULL SHOT - FROM GEORGE'S ANGLE

The Building & Loan offices are gone. The floor
formerly occupied by George's offices is now tenanted
by a guady upstairs honky-tonk. A neon sign blazens
the name: THE GROOVE. Wailing hepcat music drifts
into the street.

ANOTHER ANGLE

Behind George, at the curb, the police Black Maria
is parked. George goes over to the driver.

                    GEORGE
          Excuse me -

The cop stares into his bewildered eyes.

                    GEORGE (cont'd)
          Can you tell me where the
          Building and Loan is?

                    COP
          The building and what?

                    GEORGE
          The Bailey Building & Loan that used
          to be here.

                    COP
          Oh. They went out of business years
          ago.

George looks again toward the building. Suddenly
above the SOUND of the music, we hear a female
voice raised in shrill, drunken complaint.

                    VOICE
          Leggo! -- Lemme go - you flat-footed
          apes!

From the building a couple of cops emerge, carrying
between them the struggling, writhing figure of a
woman dressed in gaudy finery, her hair disarrayed,
her hat askew; fighting, biting and tearing as the
cops drag her out of the building toward the parked
patrol wagon.

                                   (CONTINUED)

CLOSEUP - GEORGE

He registers anguished shock as his eyes follow:

CLOSE (MOVING) SHOT - COPS AND WOMAN

As CAMERA FOLLOWS their course across the sidewalk, we recognize the screaming woman being evicted
from the honky-tonk as Violet Bick.

                    VIOLET
             (with drunken, almost
              unintelligible rage)
        I never jack-rolled anybody in my
        life! That sailor's a liar! I'm an
        American citizen - you can't do this
        to me! I know the Mayor! I know the
        Chief and every other big shot in
        town! -- The Judge is a friend of mine --
        I'll have you kicked off the force
        for this.

Unceremoniously the cops pitch her into the wagon
and as it starts away, CAMERA PANS to take in a
taxi which has been parked a few feet behind the
police car. Ernie is at the wheel of the taxi.
George comes INTO SHOT and up to Ernie.

He runs across the street to Ernie's cab and jumps in.

                    GEORGE
        Ernie, take me home, will you?
        Quick, I'm off my nut.

                    ERNIE
             (a much harder
              Ernie)
        Where do you live, Bud?

                    GEORGE
        Aw, come on now, Ernie, don't you
        get that way on me. Home - you know
        where it is - 320 Sycamore.

                    ERNIE
        Oh - 320 Syca - 320?

                    GEORGE
        Hurry up, Ernie, Zuzu's sick!

                    ERNIE
        Right.

                                    (CONTINUED)

INT. ERNIE'S CAB - PROCESS - UNBORN SEQUENCE

George jumps into cab hurriedly.

                    GEORGE
          Hurry up, Ernie- Zuzu's sick.

                    ERNIE
          All right -- Zuzu's sick.

He pulls down flag and starts off. Ernie is puzzled
by the stranger in the cab.

                    GEORGE
               (confused)
          Look, straighten me out, Ernie.
          I've got some bad liquor or something.
          You are Ernie Bishop, and you live with
          your wife and kid in Bailey Park. That's
          right, isn't it?

                    ERNIE
               (belligerently)
          You seen my wife?

                    GEORGE
               (exasperated)
          Haven't I been to your house a
          hundred times?

                    ERNIE
               (menacing tone)
          Hey, Bud, what's coming off here?
          I live in a shack in Potter's Field --
          and my wife left me three years ago --
          and took the kid -- and I ain't never
          seen you before in my life.

                    GEORGE
          Okay, okay -- faster -- faster,
          will you?

Ernie turns to driving, but he's worried about his
passenger. As he turns a corner, he sees Bert,
the cop. Attracting his attention, he motions to
Bert to follow him, indicating he has a nut in the
back. Bert starts his motor and follows.

                              (CONTINUED)

EXT. GEORGE'S HOUSE - NIGHT

Taxi and motorcycle come to a halt before house. It
is in far worse condition than when George and Mary
went to live in it in 1932. But since house is dark
we don't observe this at once.

CLOSER ANGLE.

                    ERNIE
          This the place?

                    GEORGE
               (jumping out)
          'Course it's the place.

                    ERNIE
          This house ain't been lived in for
          twenty years.

Ernie gets out. Bert stands alongside him.

                    BERT
          What's up, Ernie?

                    ERNIE
          I don't know. We better keep an eye
          on this bird - he's bats.

Ernie turns his spotlight on the house.

EXT. HOUSE

MED. SHOT - George comes into shot. He is stopped
momentarily by the appearance of the house. Windows
are broken, the porch sags, one section of roof has
fallen, door bangs open, askew on one hinge. Like
a doomed man George enters.

INT. GEORGE'S HOUSE

The interior of the house is lit up here and there,
ghostlike, by Ernie's spotlight. No furtniture,
cobwebs, wall paper hanging and swinging - stairs are
broken and collapsed. In a voice that sounds like
a cry for help, George yells out:

                    GEORGE
          Mary! Where are you, Mary?
          Peter! Janie! Zuzu! Tommy!

                                      (CONTINUED)

He starts up the broken stairway, but is stopped by
fallen portions.

                    GEORGE (cont'd)
          Where are you?

                    CLARENCE'S VOICE
          They're not here, George. You have
          no children.

CLOSEUP - Clarence. Clarence stands in the hallway,
lit up by ray from Ernie's spotlight.

Bert the cop, gun in hand stands at doorway.

                    BERT
          All right, put up your hands -
          and no fast moves. Come on outside,
          both of you.

George, hearing Bert's familiar voice runs out to
him.

                    GEORGE
          Bert, Bert! Thank Heaven you're here!

                    BERT
          Stand back!

                    GEORGE (cont'd)
          Have you seen Mary? What's happened to
          my house? Where are my kids?

EXT. GEORGE'S PORCH

George ends this speech by coming outside and grabbing
Bert's lapels.

                    ERNIE
               (standing by)
          Watch him, Bert!

                    BERT
          Now fella, take it easy. We'll go in
          town and find 'em. come on, come on.

                    GEORGE
          Bert - Ernie! My house - you two were
          here on my wedding night - you stood
          right there and sang for me - don't
          you remember?

                              (CONTINUED)

                          ERNIE
                  (becoming frightened)
              Oh oh! I'll be going.

                          BERT
                  (doubling George's
                   arm behind him)
              That's a good boy. Now let's go
              into town. We'll see the doctor -
              everything'll be all right.

                          GEORGE
              Let go of me!
                  (he struggles)
              Ernie, take me over to my mother's
              house! Bert! It's this guy here -
                  (points to Clarence)
              He says he's an angel - he's
              hypnotized me. Let me go.

George struggles to get free. Bert reverses his gun
as a club.

                          BERT
              I hate to do this, fella.

Bert lifts his gun to club George on the head. Clarence
leaps on his arm and bites his hand.

                          CLARENCE
              Run George! Run George!

In the scuffle George gets free and runs away. Bert
turns to free himself of Clarence who is hanging
on to him like a leach. In the scuffle they fall,
Bert on top. Bert reaches one hand for handcuffs.
Clarence struggles and screams.

                          CLARENCE
              Help! Joseph - help!

Ernie has been watching scene. All of a sudden his
eyes pop. He sees Bert wrestling with himself.
Clarence has disappears right from under him.

                          BERT
              Where'd he go? Where'd he go?
              I have him right here! Ernie,
              don't let that other guy get away!

                              (CONTINUED)

                        ERNIE
                  (running toward
                   his cab)
           I need a drink.

                        BERT
                  (disheveled and mad)
           Which way'd they go? We got to
           find 'em. Come on, let's get 'em.

                        ERNIE
                  (paralyzed with fear)
           They're ghosts.

                        BERT
           Come on - get in your cab!

                        ERNIE
           A cab would only be in my way!

Ernie turns and runs in opposite direction. Bert
hops on his motor and goes after George.

EXT. MA BAILEY'S HOUSE - NIGHT

A dim light burns over the door. The SOUND of
boogie-woogie piano playing can be heard faintly.
George runs up to front door. It is locked. He
rings bell. While waiting, his eye sees a sign.

CLOSEUP - sign. It reads "Room to Rent - No Vacancies!"
George turns quickly as he hears door opening. Mrs.
Bailey stands in doorway.

                        GEORGE
           Well, Mother, Mother.

The woman doesn't answer. His mother has changed
amazingly. Her face is harsh and tired. In her eyes
once kindly and understanding, there is now suspicion.
She gives no sign that she knows him.

                        MA BAILEY
                  (flatly)
           Mother! What do you want?

It is a cruel blow to George.

                                        (CONTINUED)

                              GEORGE
          Mother, don't you know me - this is
          George. I thought sure you'd
          remember me.

                              MOTHER
          George who? If you want a room there's
          no vacancy.

His mother starts to close the door. George puts
his hand on the knob, stopping her.

                              GEORGE (cont'd)
          Mother, please help me. Something's
          happened to me - to everybody - I
          don't know what. Will you let me
          keep here for a while - until I get
          over it?

                              MA BAILEY
          Get over what? I dont take in
          strangers unless they been sent here
          by somebody I know.

                              GEORGE
                  (hopefully)
          Oh, I know a lot of people you know-
          Uncle Billy, your brother-in-law...

                              MA BAILEY
          You know him?

                              GEORGE
          Sure I do.

                              MA BAILEY
          When'd you see him last?

                              GEORGE
          I saw him today - at his house.

                              MA BAILEY
          That's a lie. Bill Bailey's in an
          insane asylum since he lost his
          business -

                              GEORGE
          Insane Asylum! Uncle Billy?

                              MA BAILEY
                  (acidly)
          Yes and if you ask me, you belong there
          yourself!

                                          (CONTINUED)

She tries to slam door. George puts his foot in the
door.

>   GEORGE
>   Mom - mom - just one more thing -
>   Where can I find Mary?

>   MA BAILEY
>   Mary who?

>   GEORGE
>   My wife - Mary Bailey - she used to be
>   Mary Hatch. You must have seen her
>   hundreds of times - sne used to play
>   with your sons - went to high school
>   with them --

>   MA BAILEY
>   I only had one son - and I lost him
>   long before he went to high school.
>   You better go and sleep it off some
>   place.

She   slams   door in his face. He stands a moment
crushed. Then he turns and walks toward the curb.
He sits down on it wearily. He runs his hands through
his hair trying to pierce the impenetrable fog.

>   CLARENCE'S VOICE
>   Strange, isn't it?

George looks quickly to one side. CAMERA PULLS BACK
revealing Clarence seated alongside, munching an
apple.

>   CLARENCE (cont'd)
>   Each man's life touches so many other
>   lives - and when he's not around he
>   leaves an awful hole, doesn't he?

>   GEORGE
>   (quietly, trying to
>   use logic)
>   You're not an angel. You're a devil.
>   That's it - I've heard of these things.
>   You've got me in some kind of a spell -
>   but I'll get out of it. I know how.
>   The last man I talked to, before this
>   happened, was Martini. Yeah, that's it
>   - Martini! If I could only find
>   Martini.

>   (CONTINUED)

                         CLARENCE
          Know where he lives?

                          GEORGE
          Sure - in Bailey Park.

He gets to his feet and starts out. Clarence rises
slowly and goes after him.

                                        DISSOLVE

EXT. WALLED PARK - NIGHT

FULL SHOT. In the background we see two figures
approaching camera.

CLOSING MOVING SHOT - George and Clarence, walking
along an old shoulder-high brick wall.

                         CLARENCE
          Are you sure this is Bailey Park?

                          GEORGE
               (in a dead voice)
          I'm not sure of anything any more.
          I only know it should be Bailey Park.
               (a groan)
          But where are the houses - where are
          all the houses?

They have reached a gateway and they pause before it.

LONG SHOT - from George's point of view. We see that
the park is a cemetary.

TWO SHOT - George and Clarence. There is pity on
Clarence's face as he looks at George.

                         CLARENCE
               (gently)
          The houses are here, after all.

Without response, and walking as if in a trance,
George exits shot. Clarence follows ater him.

CLOSE MOVING SHOT - George after wandering like a lost soul
among the tombstones, Clarence trotting at his heels.
Again George stops to stare with frightened eyes at:

                                        (CONTINUED)

CLOSE SHOT - a tombstone. Upon it is engraved a
name: HARRY BAILEY. Beneath this the figures,
hyphenated, telling the birth and death date.

TWO SHOT - George and Clarence. George is so stricken
that he cannot say anything.

                    CLARENCE
               (gently)
          Harry Bailey broke through the ice and
          was drowned - at the age of nine.

                    GEORGE
          That's a lie. My kid brother went to
          war! He got the Congressional Medal
          of Honor! He saved the lives of every
          man on that transport.

                    CLARENCE
          Every man on that transport died.
          Harry wasn't there to save them,
          because you weren't there to save
          Harry.

George stares at the tombstone, then CAMERA PANS
WITH him as he walks over to it and bending, starts
to feel it with his hands, as if to reassure himself
that it is real and not a figment of his imagination.
His hands touch the bas-relief letters on the stone.
Presently George straightens and looks over toward:

CAMERA PANS across Martini family tombstone.

                    CLARENCE
          Since there was no Bailey Park, the
          Martini's never moved out of Potter's
          slums. Fire burnt down several houses
          one year.
               (George starts as this
                news sinks in)
          You see, George, you really had a
          wonderful life. Don't you see what a
          mistake it would be to throw it
          away?

                    GEORGE
          Listen you - Clarence - whatever you
          are - real or ghost -
               (grabs him)
          Where's Mary?

                                        (CONTINUED)

                        CLARENCE
        I'm not supposed to - you won't like
        it, George.

                        GEORGE
        Where is she?

                        CLARENCE
        She's an old maid - never married...

                        GEORGE
        Where is she -- tell me -- before I
        strangle you -

                        CLARENCE
        All right - all right. She's about to
        close up the library.

George throws him down and runs out. Clarence
pulls himself up, feeling his neck.

                        CLARENCE
        There must be some easier way for me
        to get my wings.

He gets up and runs after George.

CLOSEUP - Mary. She comes down library steps - a
very different Mary. No buoyancy in her walk,
none of Mary's abandon and love of life. Glasses,
no makeup, lips compressed, elbows close to body.
She looks flat and dried up, and extremely self-
satisfied and efficient.

CLOSEUP - George, as he looks at her.

MED. SHOT. Mary comes primly down and, passing right
under George's nose she starts down sidewalk. George
follows her a moment with his eyes, then calls to her.

                        GEORGE
                (softly)
        Mary! Mary!

Mary turns and looks at him.

CLOSEUP - George. In his eyes there is a desparate
appeal. If she doesn't know him, then he is lost. He
takes a couple of steps toward her.

                                        (CONTINUED)

>   GEORGE
>   Mary - it's George - George.

CLOSEUP - Mary. She stares at him blankly for a
second, then turns and hastens her steps to get away
from the fresh stranger.

MED SHOT - George overtakes her and grabs her.

>   GEORGE
>   (desperately)
>   Mary, it's me - George! Don't
>   you know me? What's happened to
>   us?

Mary, paralyzed with fright, tries to squirm away.

>   MARY
>   I don't know you - let me go!

>   GEORGE
>   Mary - don't do this to me - I need
>   you. Where are the kids? Help me,
>   Mary.

Mary suddenly finds her breath and from her lips comes
a piercing scream.

CLOSEUP - Bert the motor cop. He is parked on
corner. He hears Mary's scream and starts his
motor.

MED. SHOT - Mary struggling with George. She is now
screaming and fighting to get away.

>   GEORGE
>   Mary! Wait a minute! Wait a minute!

A couple of passersby come to Mary's rescue and hold
George's arms, temporarily allowing Mary to escape.
Shaking them off, George runs after her.

>   GEORGE
>   Mary! Mary! Don't run a way!

MED. SHOT. Mary sees him coming and runs into a
small cafe and beer parlor.

INT. BEER PARLOR

Small tables, booths, perhaps a counter. It is
crowded. Many of the people are the same who were
present during the run on the Building and Loan.

                                        (CONTINUED)

Ernie is drinking and explaining about the ghost to
a negro friend in a janitor uniform. Mary comes
running in, screaming.

                    MARY
          Help - a wild man is after me!
          Stop him! Help! He's mad!
          He's mad!

The place goes into an uproar. George comes in,
practically insane.

                    GEORGE
          Mary! Don't run away! Don't
          leave me!

Several people grab him. Others surround the
hysterical Mary. Mary's frightened cries and
George's entreaties go on together.

CLOSEUP. Ernie and Janitor in a front booth.
Ernie's eyes pop out of his head.

                    ERNIE
          That's <u>him</u>!

He turns and crashes right through the window,
followed by the janitor.

CLOSEUP. George being held back by customers.

                    GEORGE
             (recognizing some of them)
          Ed - Charlie! That's my wife -
          I want her - Mary! Mary!

                    CROWD
          Oh, no you don't! Call the
          police, somebody! Hit him with
          a bottle! Wait a minute! Give us
          a hand here! He needs a straight
          jacket.

George can't fight through them. Desparately he
thinks of Clarence.

                    GEORGE
          Clarence! Clarence! Where are
          you?
             (starts struggling to
              get away from them)

(CONTINUED)

CLOSEUP. Clarence. He is peering in through hole
in window left. On hearing George call him his face
lights up. It is apparent he has been waiting for
this.

EXT. CAFE DOOR

George dashes out and collides with Bert the motor
cop, almost knocking him down.

                         BERT
                  (recognizing him)
            Oh, it's you!

He grabs George and reaches for his gun. George lets
him have one square on the button and dashes down
street yelling:

                         GEORGE
            Clarence! Clarence!

Crowd comes rushing out of cafe. Bert comes to
quickly, and, taking out his gun fires several shots
after the fleeing George. Bert then dashes to his
motorcycle and roars after him.

CLOSEUP - Ernie in doorway talking to Clarence, who
is happily munching an apple.

                         ERNIE
                  (excitedly)
            He's a ghost, I tell you. And the
            other one was a little old guy,
            just about your -
                  (he freezes stiff as
                   he recognizes Clarence)
            YOWEE -!

He turns and runs smack into a brick wall.

                                        DISSOLVE OUT

DISSOLVE IN

EXT. BRIDGE - NIGHT

The same part of bridge where George was standing
before Clarence jumped in. The wind is blowing as
it has all through the unborn sequence. George
comes running into shot. He is frantically looking
for Clarence.

                                        (CONTINUED)

                              GEORGE
                        (shouting)
              Clarence! Where are you, Clarence?
              I want to be like I was! I want to
              be born again! I don't care what I
              have to face - scandal - prison -
              anything - only get me back to my
              wife and kids! Let me live again!
              Clarence - get me back! Get me back!

Suddenly toward the end of the above the wind dies
down. A soft, gentle snow begins to fall. O.s.
George hears the roar and siren of a motorcycle. A
searchlight hits George squarely in the face.

ANOTHER ANGLE - SHOOTING TOWARD town. Bert on
his motorcycle comes roaring toward George. Bert
stops, leaps off his motor and approaches George.

                              BERT
              George, George! What's the matter?

                              GEORGE
                        (menacingly)
              Stay away from me! I'll hit you again!
              Clarence! Clarence! Get me back!
              Get me back!

                              BERT
                        (closer to him)
              George! What the Sam Hill you
              yelling about! George!

                              GEORGE
              Don't come near me - <u>George</u>?
              You know me? Bert - you know me?

                              BERT
              Are you kiddin', George? Are you
              all right? I've been looking all over
              for you. Found your car smashed up a
              tree, and I was afraid -- your mouth's
              bleeding.

George's rapture knows no bounds.

                              GEORGE
              Oh boy, my mouth's bleeding!
              He knows me!
                        (searches his
                        pocket)
              Zuzu's petals - they're here,
              Bert - they're here! Merry Christmas,
              Bert, Merry Christmas!

                                              (CONTINUED)

He practically embraces the astonished Bert. Then
runs at top speed toward town.

LONG   SHOT - George runs away from camera yelling:

                    GEORGE
          Mary! Mary!

MED. SHOT - scarred tree. George runs into shot,
sees wrecked car - stops in his flight to look for
scar on tree. It's there. George is grateful.
He kisses scar on tree and runs on.

MED. SHOT - house. Owner of tree sees George and
yells at him.

                    OWNER
          Hey you!

                    GEORGE
               (over his shoulder)
          Merry Christmas!

EXT. MAIN STREET - NIGHT

CLOSE TRUCKING SHOT - George runs through Main Street
on way home. As he runs he joyfully notices town
is back where it was. "Pottersville" signs have
been replaced by "Bedford Falls." He sees SHOTS
of:

MOVING SHOT - GOWER'S DRUGSTORE

MOVING SHOT - BEDFORD FALLS BANK

MOVING SHOT - BUILDING AND LOAN

CLOSEUP - George running. As he sees these things he
shouts "Merry Christmas" at random. As he goes by
Potter's Bank he sees Potter looking out of his
lighted window.

                    GEORGE
               (at window)
          Hey Mr. Potter - Merry Christmas!
          Mr. Potter!

                                        (CONTINUED)

INT. POTTER'S OFFICE. The goon goes to window,
looks out after George.

                    POTTER
          And a happy New Year in jail. Go on
          home - they're waiting for you.
               (to goon)
          Well, I can go home now - go get
          the carriage.

As the goon exits Potter suddenly sees Clarence seated
in a chair, calmy munching an apple.

                    POTTER (cont'd)
          Who are you? How'd you get in here?
          What are you doing?

                    CLARENCE
          Don't really know, myself. You're none
          of my business, you know. Joseph won't
          like it, either.

Potter reaches for telephone.

                    CLARENCE (cont'd)
          Uh, uh. I wouldn't call the police.
          Besides if they come I'd have to tell
          them of the money you stole from Uncle
          Billy.

Potter's hand leaves phone.

                    CLARENCE (cont'd)
          That was a wicked thing to do. It
          not only made you a thief; it almost
          made you a murderer. You almost killed
          George Bailey tonight.
               (looking up)
          Coming. I'm not going to Coney Island.
          Coming! Are you going to let this old
          stinkpot get away with this?
               (to Potter)
          You're an old man, Henry Potter; bitter,
          selfish and lonely. You're going to die
          soon - then what? Can you think of any
          one in the world - man, woman, child
          or animal that would care? Think
          hard, Potter, are you the richest man
          around here, or the poorest?

Clarence disappears, leaving the core of his apple.

                                        (CONTINUED)

CLOSE SHOT - Potter at desk.

                    POTTER
              (yelling)
         Help! Horace - help! Help!
         Horace! Help!

                              DISSOLVE OUT

DISSOLVE IN
EXT. GEORGE BAILEY'S HOME - NIGHT

The house is now lit up and back to normal. George
comes dashing into shot and stops just a moment to
take in the joyous sight. Then he bolts into the
house.

INT. DOWNSTAIRS - GEORGE'S HOUSE

Bank examiner, a deputy and a couple of reporters are
in hallway downstairs as door opens and George bursts
in.

                    GEORGE
         Hello you draughty old house!
         MARY! MARY! Hi, Mr. Bank Examiner!

                    CARTER
         Mr. Bailey -- there's a deficit.

                    GEORGE
              (very gay)
         I know - I know. Eight thousand dollars.
         Right?

                    DEPUTY
         George - we've got a little paper
         here.

                    GEORGE
         Isn't that wonderful? Warrant for my
         arrest. I'm going to jail! Merry
         Christmas!
              (runs toward
               kitchen)
         MARY! MARY!
              (dashes back
               into hallway)
         Anybody seen my wife?

                              (CONTINUED)

Children come out onto upstairs landing.

                         CHILDREN
              Merry Christmas, daddy! Merry
              Christmas, Dad!

George runs upstairs.

                         GEORGE
              Peter - Janie - Tommy!

MED SHOT - TOP OF STAIRS. George runs up to the
children and sweeps them into his arms, almost
crushing them. The kids scream with delight.

                         GEORGE
              Peter! Janie! Tommy! I'm going to
              eat all of you. Ummmmmm. Why aren't
              you all in bed?

                         JANIE
              We were in bed.

                         PETER
              We heard a noise downstairs.

                         TOMMY
              We thought it might be Santa.

                         GEORGE
              Where's Mother?

                         PETER
              She went out looking for you.

                         JANIE
              With Uncle Billy.

                         PETER
              Where you been?

                         GEORGE
              A long way off, Pete.

From adjoining room comes Zuzu's voice.

                         ZUZU'S VOICE
              Daddy! Daddy!

                                    (CONTINUED)

INT. HALLWAY - UPSTAIRS

Little Zuzu comes flying toward her daddy. She is
in her bedclothes.

MED. SHOT - George catches her.

                         GEORGE
              Zuzu! My little gingersnap.
                    (he sits on the top
                      step crushing her to him)
              How do you feel?

                         ZUZU
              Fine, Daddy.

                         JANIE
              Not a smitch of temperature.

                         GEORGE
              Hallelujah! How do you spell it,
              Pete?

INT. HALLWAY - DOWNSTAIRS

Carter and a man from the District Attorney's office
look on with open mouths as they see an hysterial
father kiss and feel and crush his four children.

MED. SHOT - doorway. The door bursts open. Mary
enters breathless and excited.

                         MARY
                    (to two men)
              Hello.
                    (then she spots George
                      at top of stairs)
              George! Darling! Where have you
              been -- ?

She runs up the stairs. He runs down. They meet in
a fierce embrace.

                         GEORGE
              Mary! Let me touch you - you're real -
              you're real!
                    (covers her with kisses,
                      Mary trying to talk at
                      same time, but he won't
                      let her)

                                           (CONTINUED)

                         GEORGE (cont'd)
          You have no idea what happened to me --

                         MARY
          You have no idea what happened to <u>me</u>.
                    (takes him by
                     a hand)
          Come down here, quick. They're
          coming now.

                         GEORGE
          Who's coming? What? Who?
          Where are you going?

INT. LIVING ROOM

Mary leads George into living room and stands him
near the Christmas tree. The kids trail in too.

                         MARY
               Stand right there - by the Christmas
               tree. You'll see. I hear 'em now.
               It's a miracle George.

She runs toward front door and flings it open. Ad
lib SOUNDS of an excited crowd can be heard. Uncle
Billy, face flushed, covered with snow, and carrying
a clothes basket filled with money, bursts in. He
is followed by Ernie, and about twenty more
townspeople.

                         MARY (cont'd)
               In here, Uncle Billy. Come right in
               everybody!
                    (points to living room)

                         UNCLE BILLY
          Bushelsful, Mary! Bushelsful!

INT. LIVING ROOM

Uncle Billy, Mary and crowd come into living room.
A table stands in front of George. George picks up
Zuzu to protect her. Uncle Billy dumps basketful of
money on table. It overflows and falls all over.

                         UNCLE BILLY
               George - you never saw anything like
               it -- you never saw anything like it!

                                        (CONTINUED)

The rest of the crowd all greet George with greetings
and smiles. Each one comes forward with money. In
their pockets, in shoe boxes, in coffee pots. Money
pours on the table - pennies, dimes, quarters, dollar
bills - small money, but lots of it. Mrs. Bailey and
Mrs. Hatch push toward George. More people come in.
The place becomes a bedlam. Shouts of "Gangway -
gangway" as a new bunch comes in and pours out its
money. Gower comes in with an apothecary jar full.
Annie comes in. Martini comes in with Mrs. Martini.
All the people we've met. Violet Bick comes in
with the money George loaned her. The house fills
up. Throughout this there is ad lib chatter directed
to George.

                    AD LIBS
          Glad to do it, George.
          If it wasn't for you, I'd had
          no roof over my head.
          Any old time for you, George.

Mary stands next to George watching him. George stands
there overcome and speechless as he holds Zuzu. As
he sees the familiar faces, he gives them sick grins.
Tears course down his face. His lips frame their
names as he greets them.

                    PARTRIDGE
               (the school principal)
          Here you are, George -- had to
          get the whole faculty out of
          bed, but here you are!

                    KEAN
          What's this - another run on the bank?

                    MR. MARTINI
          I got all the money out of the
          cash register -- and I broke the
          juke box, too!

                    MR. GOWER
          I made the rounds of all my charge
          accounts.

                    VIOLET
          George, I decided to stick around.

                    ANNIE
          I've been saving this for a
          divorce -- if ever I get a husband.

                    (CONTINUED)

MR. WELCH
I'm sorry, George. It was all a mistake.

INSERT   As people crowd in, one of them hands a wire
          to Mary; she opens it, reads it, passes it
          on to Ernie who shushes every one and
          reads: "MR. GOWER CABLED YOU NEED CASH.
          MY OFFICE INSTRUCTED TO ADVANCE UP TO TWENTY-
          FIVE THOUSAND DOLLARS. HEE-HAW AND A MERRY
          XMAS. SAM WAINWRIGHT."

UNCLE BILLY
(emotionally at the
breaking point)
Mary did it, George! You never saw
anything like it! She told a few
people you were in trouble and then --
like a prairie fire, George, people
scattered through the town collecting
money. No questions asked -- all they
say was "If George's in trouble,
count on me." Nickels, dimes dollars --
you never saw anything like it --
(breaks)
--a miracle-- all these friends --
We're saved, George -- We're saved!

Uncle Billy very quietly moves behind the Christmas
tree, and utters a low prayer of thanksgiving.

NEW ANGLE - Mary.

She suddenly looks at clock.

MARY
Janie - the piano, it's almost twelve!
We've got punch, everybody! Mother,
Annie -- glasses. Mr. Martini, how
about some wine!

Janie hops to the piano and begins playing the
Christmas carol she had been practicing. Ernie picks
it up and soon all are singing "Hark The Herald
Angels Sing". Annie and Cousin Tilly are busy passing
out the punch.

HARRY
Hello, George, Mary -- Looks like I
got here too late.

(CONTINUED)

> BERT
> Mary, I got him here from the airport
> as quick as I could. He flew all
> the way up in a blizzard.

> MRS. BAILEY
> Harry, what about your banquet in New York?

> HARRY
> Left right in the middle -- soon as
> I got Mary's wire --
> (takes glass)
> To my big brother George -- the
> richest man in town!

As Harry toasts his brother, Bert starts playing
"Auld Lang Syne" on his accordion and again, every
one breaks into song.

INT. LIVING ROOM

CLOSE SHOT on George, still holding Zuzu, glances
down at pile of presents under tree. His eye catches
something on top of pile. He reaches for it. It
is Clarence's copy of "Tom Sawyer". George recognizes
it. He opens it and finds an inscription written in
it.

CLOSEUP - flyleaf of book.

> "Dear George -- This is to remember
> me by, and to remember this: <u>no</u>
> man is a failure who has friends.
> Thanks for the wings. Love, Clarence."

MED. SHOT - as George stares at inscription. Mary
comes into shot.

> MARY
> What's that, darling?

> GEORGE
> Present. A Christmas present from
> a very dear friend.

Mary takes it and reads it. Perhaps it is the
jostling by some of the people on the other side of
the Christmas tree, but a little bell on one of the
limbs next to George's head begins to tinkle as it
swings to and fro.

(CONTINUED)

                         ZUZU
          Look, daddy --
               (points to bell)
          Teacher says every time a bell
          rings some angel gets his wings.

George nods vigorously. Then he looks up, and shaking
a congratulatory head, his eyes and his smile say,
"Attaboy, Clarence". The voices of the people singing
swell into a final crescendo for the

                                   FADE OUT

          THE END